Tools for Young Philosophers

Tools for Young Philosophers

The Elements of Philosophy

PAUL TIMOTHY JENSEN

WIPF & STOCK · Eugene, Oregon

TOOLS FOR YOUNG PHILOSOPHERS
The Elements of Philosophy

Copyright © 2011 P. T. Jensen. All rights reserved. Except for brief quotations in critical publications or reviews, no part of this book may be reproduced in any manner without prior written permission from the publisher. Write: Permissions, Wipf and Stock Publishers, 199 W. 8th Ave., Suite 3, Eugene, OR 97401.

Wipf & Stock
An Imprint of Wipf and Stock Publishers
199 W. 8th Ave., Suite 3
Eugene, OR 97401
www.wipfandstock.com

ISBN 13: 978-1-61097-691-6
Manufactured in the U.S.A.

*To the memory of Louis Frederick Jensen
Soldier, Husband, Pastor, Father, Missionary, Friend
Life-long student and lover of books and ideas*

Contents

Preface xi
Acknowledgments xiii

1 SCIENCE AND PHILOSOPHY 1

2 LOGIC 4
    Premise and Conclusion
    Deduction and Induction
    Valid and Sound
    Fallacy
    Laws of thought
        Non-contradiction
        Identity
        Excluded middle
    Necessary and Sufficient
    Theoretical and Practical Reasoning

3 EPISTEMOLOGY 20
    Belief and Knowledge
    Truth and Falsehood
        Necessary and Contingent
            —A priori and A posteriori
            —Analytic and Synthetic

        The Pragmatic Theory of Truth
        The Coherence Theory of Truth
        The Correspondence Theory of Truth
        The Realist Theory of Truth

Rationalism and Empiricism
Realism and Anti-Realism

4 METAPHYSICS 37
Universal and Particular
Substance and Property
Realism and Idealism
Body and Mind
Existence and Essence
Essential and Accidental
Free Will and Determinism
Compatibilism and Incompatibilism
Four Aristotelian Causes
Material Cause
Formal Cause
Efficient Cause
Final Cause
Difference in Degree and Difference in Kind

5 MORAL PHILOSOPHY/ETHICS 58
Is and Ought
Right and Wrong
Good and Evil
Natural Law
Deontology
Consequentialism
Virtue Ethics
Divine Command Ethics
Euthyphro Dilemma
Rights

6 ANALYTIC PHILOSOPHY AND CONTINENTAL
   PHILOSOPHY 78

7 GREAT PHILOSOPHERS YOU SHOULD KNOW 83
   Socrates (469–399 BC)
   Plato (427–347 BC)
   Aristotle (384–322 BC)
   Augustine (354–430)
   Anselm (1033–1109)
   Aquinas (1225–1274)
   Descartes (1596–1650)
   Locke (1632–1704)
   Kant (1724–1804)
   Hegel (1770–1831)
   Heidegger (1889–1976)
   Wittgenstein (1889–1951)

Bibliography 131
Subject/Name Index 139

Preface

THE LIBERAL arts liberate our minds and the humanities humanize us. Philosophy, as part of the liberal arts and as one of the humanities, can do both. The way to begin your liberation and humanization is by learning the most basic philosophical concepts, a task less difficult than you might think. If you are an aspiring young philosopher or just curious about philosophy, this book will give you a jump start. In about three hours of reading time, you will become familiar with the most basic building blocks of philosophy and will become acquainted with twelve of the most influential philosophers in western history. To make the information as memorable as possible, many of the terms are arranged in pairs so that you get two for the price of one and can quickly grasp how they are related.

Philosophers use many other terms in addition to those explained in this book, but if you don't learn the most basic ones you will miss interesting and important things written by them over the past twenty-five hundred years. Other disciplines in the humanities use many of the same terms, and so by mastering them you will also obtain tools for understanding historians, sociologists, psychologists, economists, and political scientists. You may even acquire the ability to articulate your own agreement or disagreement with what you have read, and that would indicate that you are making major strides in being humanized and liberated.

I hope you find yourself asking questions as you read. If you are a college student, take your questions first to your professors who are being paid to encourage you to formulate and think about hard questions. But you should also feel free to contact me at PJensen@dbq.edu.

Acknowledgments

David Hill at Augustana College, Roman Ciapalo at Loras College, and Roger Ebertz at the University of Dubuque gave me my first, second, and third opportunities to teach philosophy to undergraduates. I am deeply grateful to each of them for permitting me to do what, next to being a husband and father, I love best. During the past twenty or so years of teaching, I have also learned a great deal from the many hundreds of students who have listened to lectures, entered into class discussions, and studied for exams—my sincere thanks to each of them.

Matt Jensen read the entire manuscript and Ben Jensen read a portion of it. Both made serious suggestions for improving clarity, some of which I initially resisted, but all of which I eventually acknowledged to be improvements and so incorporated. My thanks also to Rachel Jensen, and to my wife Sharon, for their love and encouragement.

1

Science and Philosophy

NEARLY SIX centuries before the birth of Jesus of Nazareth, Thales of Miletus (born c. 624 BC) gained fame in the Greek world by making an extraordinary prediction. The ancient historian Herodotus claimed that "The Ionians received a prediction of (an) eclipse from Thales of Miletus, who had determined that this was the year in which an eclipse would occur."[1] In the twenty-first century, predicting a solar eclipse would fall within the jurisdiction of science not philosophy; nevertheless, when Thales' prediction came true, he gained the designation of being the first philosopher, not the first scientist. The reason for this curious fact is that during most of the past two thousand five hundred years, all human knowledge was part of "philosophy."[2]

The distinction between science as we know it and philosophy is recent. The Latin root of the English word "science" is *scire*, which means "to know." During the Middle Ages, any specific body of knowledge, even theology, was

---

1. Herodotus, *The Landmark Herodotus: The Histories*, 1.74.2, 42. This solar eclipse has been dated to May 23, 585 BC.

2. Laertius, *Lives of the Eminent Philosophers*, Vol. 1, 23. "He was the first to receive the name of Sage, in the archonship of Damasias at Athens, when the term was applied to all the Seven Sages . . ."

called a science. What today we call science was known in the Middle Ages as "natural philosophy," and this explains why a person in the twenty-first century who earns a terminal degree in biology, chemistry, or physics is awarded a "doctor of philosophy" degree (PhD).[3]

Science in the modern sense can be distinguished from philosophy by considering the difference between a scientific question and a philosophical question. A scientific question can only be answered by some kind of human observation, whereas, " . . . a philosopher's job is to find out things about the world by thinking rather than observing."[4]

With this in mind, the following questions are scientific:

1. What is the atomic weight of hydrogen?

2. What is the speed of light?

3. What effect will a change in the price of gasoline have on consumption?

Question (1) is from the science of chemistry, question (2) is from physics, and question (3) is from economics, one of the social sciences. Unless you make observations about the natural world, these questions can't be answered. Of course, modern scientists must *think* in order to answer these questions, but no amount of *thinking* alone will provide accurate answers.

3. The D in PhD refers to the word doctor, which in Latin means teacher, and the Ph refers to the word philosophy, which in Greek means love of wisdom.

4. Russell, *History of Western Philosophy*, 402. Russell makes this comment in the course of his discussion of Anselm's ontological argument for God's existence. See 7.5 Anselm.

The following questions are philosophical:

4. Is torture always wrong?
5. Is a person responsible for her action if she did what she wanted to do?
6. If p implies q and q is, in fact, false, does it follow with necessity that p is also false?

Question (4) is from moral philosophy or ethics, question (5) is from metaphysics, and question (6) is from logic. Observing the natural world won't answer these questions. Of course, philosophers must know what torture is in order to give a sensible answer to question (4), but it makes no sense to suppose they must observe thirty acts of torture under controlled circumstances to determine the wrongness of torture. Similarly, (5) requires that philosophers grasp the difference between a voluntary human action (e.g., pulling the trigger of a gun) and an involuntary motion of the body (e.g., the beating of a heart). It also requires an understanding of the meaning of the word *responsible* (say, to be rightly praised or blamed) and all this results from prior experience or education. But the question itself can't be answered by making observations; it can only be answered by thinking.

The priority of thinking over observation is not unique to philosophy. It applies to mathematics as well, but mathematicians use symbols and numerals to think about quantities and their relations (adding, subtracting, multiplying and dividing), whereas philosophers use concepts and propositions to think about matters important to human well-being that aren't accessible to experiment and observation (rightness, responsibility, necessity, beliefs, truth, and the like).

2

Logic

YOU POSSESS the mental ability to infer one proposition from another. From the proposition *Jack is a father*, you infer that *Jack is a male* and that *Jack has children*. This ability—call it the power of logical inference—distinguishes you from even the higher primates and has at least three components.

First, humans have the power to *conceive* as well as *perceive*. Chimpanzees, our close animal relatives, are able to *perceive* (colors, sounds, smells, etc.), but there is no reason to think they can *conceive* (form concepts and discern meaning, etc.). The distinction may be illustrated by the difference between hearing a loud sound and understanding the concepts of sound or loudness.

Second, you have the power to formulate propositions. A chimp may sense that danger is near when it hears a sound, but cannot formulate the proposition "I hear the sound of a gun" or the proposition "Danger is near." This is because, unlike the human brain, the chimp brain does not generate language.

Third, when the powers of conceiving and formulating propositions are combined, the ability to infer one proposition from another emerges. You and a chimp may both hear the sound of a gun and run away in fright, but only you will be able to explain later that the *reason* you knew you were in danger was *because* you heard the sound of a gun. Giving an explanation requires the power of logic. You must *conceive* of the concepts *danger* and *gun*, then correctly place them within propositions, and, finally, assert that because one proposition is true another one is also true. *I heard a gun, so, I knew I was in danger.*

Making an inference or drawing a conclusion is the central feature of logic. This power develops as you mature intellectually, but almost everyone benefits from formal training. What follow are the most basic concepts and distinctions you need in order to make progress in logic.

Try the following problem before reading the footnote below. Which of the following four propositions can be inferred from the proposition: *Chicago, Illinois has paved roads*?[1]

1. Illinois is in the United States.

2. Chicago has roads.

3. Within the state of Illinois, there is a city named Chicago.

4. The Mississippi River borders Illinois.

PREMISE AND CONCLUSION

Suppose that while camping you awake in the morning and smell bacon cooking. Your mind forms the proposition "I smell bacon cooking," and from it you infer "Breakfast is being prepared." The proposition "I smell bacon cooking"

---

[1]. If you said 2 and 3, you are correct. Propositions 1 and 4 are both true, but are not true *because* Chicago, Illinois has paved roads.

serves as a *premise* and "Breakfast is being prepared" is the *conclusion*. The *premise* is the reason you draw the *conclusion* or the evidence for it. If asked, "Why do you think breakfast is being prepared?" you could reasonably reply, "Because I smell bacon cooking."

The combination of at least one premise and a conclusion is called an *argument*. Philosophy dependents on arguments, which should not be confused with quarrels. Thinking about morality, for example, requires careful consideration of arguments, and this can't be accomplished without separating premises from conclusions. Many arguments have more than one premise, such as the following:

> When persons are tortured, they experience physical or mental pain. Unlike the pain caused by surgery to remove a tumor, this pain has no benefit whatsoever to those who experience it. Inflicting gratuitous physical or mental pain degrades and dehumanizes any person. Degrading and dehumanizing persons is always morally wrong. So, torture is always wrong.

In this argument, the last sentence is the conclusion and the first four sentences are the premises. The premises are the reasons for drawing the conclusion. One mark of an educated person is the ability to distinguish the premises of an argument from its conclusion. Once you can do that, you are ready to evaluate the argument itself and you may find an argument like the one above either persuasive or unpersuasive. Evaluating an argument, however, can only take place after you can correctly identify the conclusion and after you grasp that premises are offered as evidence for the conclusion.

DEDUCTION AND INDUCTION

Arguments are divided into two general categories based on the way premises are connected to the conclusion. This connection, called the inference, is a kind of mental glue. One brand of glue we call *probability* and the other we call *necessity*. When premises are glued to the conclusion by probability, the argument is *inductive*. When premises are glued to the conclusion by necessity, the argument is *deductive*.

Although the bond created by necessity would appear to be stronger than the bond created by probability, in many instances the only glue available is probability. When meteorologists predict the weather, they must use probability, and therefore, their arguments are inductive. They say, for example:

> We see a cold weather front moving toward us at an average speed of eight miles an hour. Snow flurries are coming with it. So, there is a 90 percent likelihood that we will have snow tomorrow morning.

This argument, which attempts to predict the future, has two premises and a conclusion. Because no human knows the future with certainty, any attempt to predict it must be a matter of probability, and therefore of induction. Most of the time, we're grateful for weather predictions, despite the probabilistic nature of the conclusions. More importantly, without the power of induction, none of us would have learned to survive in our dangerous world.

Consider another argument:

> My dining room table has four legs and my dining room chairs all have four legs as well. The dining room table and matching chairs are the only furniture in my dining room. So, each piece of furniture in my dining room has at least three legs.

If the premises are true, the conclusion follows with necessity; the conclusion can't possibly be false when the premises are true. So, this is a simple deductive argument.

You can easily grasp the difference between probability and necessity, but a warning is now in order regarding deduction and induction. Some dictionaries or other works of reference describe deductive arguments as those that proceed from general premises (All men are mortal, Socrates is a man) to particular conclusions (So, Socrates is mortal). Conversely, these same reference works describe inductive arguments as those that proceed from particular premises (The sun rose in the east the day before yesterday, it rose in the east yesterday, and it rose in the east today) to general conclusions (So, the sun will always rise in the east).[2] These definitions can't be permitted to stand, because they are incomplete. Some deductive arguments do move from general to particular, and some inductive arguments move from particular to general. But simple examples are readily available that go the opposite way. Consider first this argument:

1. Most Congressmen have attended law school.
2. Alfred E. Neuman is a Congressman.
3. So, Alfred E. Neuman has probably attended law school.

---

2. See for example Jones and Wilson, *An Incomplete Education*, 329–30. Standard logic textbooks don't make this error.

Now, compare the following argument:
4. George H. W. Bush attended Yale.
5. Bill Clinton attended Yale.
6. George W. Bush attended Yale.
7. Barrack Obama attended Columbia.
8. So, all of the past four presidents attended Ivy League Schools.

You can see that in the first argument the premises are glued to the conclusion by probability, although they move from general to particular. Conversely, although the premises in the second argument move from particular to general, they are glued to the conclusion by necessity. You won't be mistaken in distinguishing deduction from induction so long as you focus on the difference between the glue of necessity and the glue of probability: probability indicates induction and necessity indicates deduction.

VALID AND SOUND

When an argument is deductive, two additional concepts are used to judge its merits. The first is *validity*—a rather difficult concept to define. One view of validity claims that a deductive argument is valid if it possesses a kind of *formal structure* in which the conclusion follows from the premises with necessity. But there are two problems with this definition.

First, it seems to equate validity with deduction. If that were the case, we should state that validity and deduction are just the same thing. But logicians don't mean that. Equating validity and deduction implies that a non-deductive argument is invalid, which is false. When the conclusion of an argument fails to follow from the premises with necessity, the argument is not always invalid; it may be inductive, using the glue of probability. The following argument uses induction and validity doesn't apply to it.

9. Most Wagnerian opera singers are corpulent.

10. Sophie is a Wagnerian opera singer.

11. So, Sophie is likely to be corpulent.

The second problem with defining validity in terms of form is that many obviously valid arguments lack a valid form that can be specified. For example, the following argument, which I will call (A), is obviously valid:

12. No person is a vegetable. (No X is a Y.)

13. So, no person is a carrot. (No X is a Z.)

Whereas, the following argument, which I will call (B), is invalid although it has an identical form:

14. No dog is a cat. (No X is a Y.)

15. So, no dog is a four-legged animal. (No X is a Z.)

A better way to understand validity is to define an argument as valid *if and only if it is impossible for the premises to be true while the conclusion is false.*[3] This explains why argument (A) is valid: if "no person is a vegetable" is true, it's impossible for "no person is a carrot" to be false. It also explains why argument (B) is invalid: if "No dog is a cat" is true, it is still possible for "No dog is a four-legged animal" to be false. Thus, the definition also enables us to formulate the very important principle of invalidity, namely, *no argument with true premises and a false conclusion is valid.* It's impossible to infer falsehood validly from truth.

3. Smith, *An Introduction to Formal Logic*, 44.

Our definition of validity is as good as we're going to get. Unfortunately, it poses an interesting problem. Suppose someone offers the following argument, which I will call (C):

16. Kim is a theist.

17. Kim is an atheist.

18. So, Kim is a male.

Pretty obviously (C) fits the definition of validity because it's impossible for the conclusion to be false while the premises are true, since the premises are contradictory. But it seems strongly counter-intuitive to consider this argument valid. Perhaps we should just ignore this or considering it an odd consequence with which we have to live.[4]

Soundness is much easier to define though harder to illustrate. An argument is sound if it possesses two attributes: validity and true premises. This combination infallibly results in a true conclusion, but we don't define *soundness* as "having a true conclusion," in part, because unsound arguments can have true conclusions as well. The difficulty in judging soundness is often a consequence of the disputed nature of a particular premise. For example, one who affirms the truth of the premise "God is a perfect being" might be inclined also to affirm the soundness of the following argument:

19. All perfect beings exist.

20. God is a perfect being.

21. So, God exists.

4. See the excellent discussion of validity in Smith, *An Introduction to Formal Logic*, 44–49.

However, anyone who denied the truth of the second premise would also deny the argument's soundness.

FALLACY

A fallacy causes an argument to fail. The words *fallacy* and *fail* both stem from the Latin word *fallere*, meaning to deceive. Fallacies cause mischief because they prevent premises from bonding to a conclusion, but may permit the argument to deceive us anyway.

A *formal fallacy* inhibits the bond of necessity in a deductive argument. Consider the following:

22. If I'm in Chicago, then I'm in Illinois.

23. I'm not in Chicago.

24. So, I'm not in Illinois.[5]

The conclusion doesn't follow from the premises because the argument commits the fallacy of *denying the antecedent*.

An *informal fallacy* inhibits the inferential bond in either a deductive or inductive argument. Consider the following:

25. Dogs emit a sound called a bark.

26. Bark can be set on fire.

27. So, some sounds can be set on fire.

---

5. Any statement of the form "If . . . then . . ." is a conditional statement. In the conditional statement *If I'm in Chicago, then I'm in Illinois*, the antecedent is "I'm in Chicago" and the consequent is "I'm in Illinois."

The conclusion doesn't follow from the premises because the argument uses the word "bark" in two different senses and thus commits the fallacy of *equivocation*.

Consider another argument:

28. The starting five players for the university basketball team were each voted high school all-Americans.
29. Each of them is excellent at his individual position.
30. So, the university will likely have an excellent team this year.

The conclusion doesn't follow from the premises because it attributes *excellence*, a property belonging to each part of the team (the individual players), to the whole team. In this case, the argument commits the fallacy of *composition*. As many coaches have learned, individual talent does *not* inevitably translate into team success. When an argument persuades while committing a fallacy, it persuades by deception. Familiarity with the most common formal and informal fallacies can arm you against various kinds of deceptions.[6]

---

6. All introductory logic books will have explanations of formal fallacies, such as denying the antecedent and affirming the consequent, and of informal fallacies, such as appeal to pity, *ad hominem*, equivocation, composition, division, sweeping and hasty generalizations, and begging the question. The fact that journalists now routinely use the phrase "begs the question" to mean "raises the question" shows how few of them took an introductory logic course.

LAWS (PRINCIPLES) OF THOUGHT[7]

From ancient times, philosophers have referred to three "laws" or "principles of thought." Usually these are called the principles of non-contradiction, identity, and excluded middle. Each can be articulated as either a metaphysical principle (referring to things) or an epistemological principle (referring to propositions).

Non-contradiction

METAPHYSICAL FORMULATION: NOTHING BOTH IS AND IS NOT SIMULTANEOUSLY.

EPISTEMOLOGICAL FORMULATION: NO STATEMENT CAN BE BOTH TRUE AND FALSE SIMULTANEOUSLY.

Plato appealed to the law of non-contradiction when he wrote that nothing will make us believe "the same thing can be, do or undergo opposites at the same time, in the same respect, and in relation to the same thing."[8] Aristotle claimed that "the firmest principle of all is one about which it is impossible to be mistaken . . . this principle is: that it is impossible for the same thing both to belong and not to belong at the same time to the same thing and in the same respect . . . "[9]

---

7. A good discussion of these principles in a modern logic text can be found in Copi and Cohen, *Introduction to Logic*, 9th ed., 372–74.

8. Cooper, *Plato: Complete Works*, 436e–437 Later Plato says: "It can't be, we say, that the same thing, with the same part of itself, in relation to the same, at the same time, does opposite things." 439b (1070)

9. Aristotle, *Metaphysics,* (1005b 10–20).

Identity

METAPHYSICAL FORMULATION: WHAT IS, IS.

EPISTEMOLOGICAL FORMULATION: IF ANY STATEMENT IS TRUE, THEN IT IS TRUE.

Could a rational person be mistaken about this? It's hard to see how. No dialogue can occur between two people unless both accept the truth of the principle of identity. If someone were seriously to deny this principle, changing the subject politely would be the best procedure. Before doing that, however, you might take a stab at offering an illustration such as "If the United States is in North America, then the United States is in North America." Or, if "Aristotle was the teacher of Alexander the Great" is true, then "Aristotle was the teacher of Alexander the Great." If anyone objects to these, waste no more time. Talk to someone else.

Excluded middle

METAPHYSICAL FORMULATION: SOMETHING EITHER IS OR IT IS NOT.

EPISTEMOLOGICAL FORMULATION: ANY STATEMENT IS EITHER TRUE OR FALSE.

Among the three principles, this is the most interesting and controversial. The advent of quantum mechanics in the twentieth century placed this principle in doubt among some theoretical physicists because of the behavior of subatomic particles. Some philosophers also have argued that, if true, the principle leads to fatalism. For example, the proposition "I will eat lunch tomorrow" seems, by the principle of excluded middle, to be either true or false. If true, it appears that no matter what choices I make between now and tomorrow, it is fated that I will eat lunch tomorrow. This poses an interesting problem which various philosophers from Aristotle onwards have discussed. Without offering a definitive solution, the principle can be articulated in a modest way that avoids fatalism. The principle means simply that any statement of the form "Either I will each lunch tomorrow or I will not each lunch tomorrow" is always true. And that is neither controversial nor doubtful.

NECESSARY AND SUFFICIENT

Philosophers frequently use the distinction between a necessary and a sufficient condition. You can easily understand this distinction. Consider again the conditional statement: *if I'm in Chicago, then I'm in Illinois*. Being in Chicago is a sufficient condition for being in Illinois. To be present in Illinois, all you need is to arrive in Chicago. It's enough; it's sufficient. But, it isn't necessary, because you could be in dozens of other cities and still be in Illinois. Conversely, being in Illinois is necessary for being in Chicago. *Only if* you are in Illinois can you be in Chicago.

Sometimes philosophers combine the two conditions by asserting that some X is both necessary and sufficient for some Y. Receiving a majority of electoral votes is both necessary and sufficient to be elected president of the United States.[10] Whereas, receiving a majority of the popular vote

---

10. Note that receiving a majority of electoral votes is neither necessary nor sufficient to *be* president of the United States, only to be *elected* president.

is neither necessary nor sufficient to be elected president of the United States. Sometimes philosophers will express the relation of being both necessary and sufficient by using a different locution. They will say, Y is the case, *if, and only if*, X is the case. Person Z has been elected president of the United States, if, and only if, she has received a majority of the electoral votes. Note further that sometimes *iff* abbreviates the phrase *if and only if*.

THEORETICAL REASONING AND PRACTICAL REASONING

As humans, we reason our way both to truth and to action. The first kind of reasoning philosophers call *theoretical* and the second they call *practical*.[11] According to Robert Audi, "practical reasoning is guided by a search for appropriate action, say action that will end a quarrel; theoretical reasoning is guided by a search for appropriate knowledge, or at least belief, say as to who wrote an anonymous note."[12]

In this regard, note that some arguments end with conclusions offered for your belief.

20. Cutting off a person's hand as punishment for stealing is cruel.

21. Cruel actions are evil.

22. So, cutting off a person's hand as punishment for stealing is evil.

---

11. Aristotle suggested that we also reason about what to make; hence, he urged that all thought is "either practical or productive or theoretical . . . " *Metaphysics*, Bk VI 1025b (25–26).

12. Audi, *Practical Reasoning*, 103.

23. I promised to take Jane to the airport.

24. Those who make promises have a duty to keep them.

25. So, I have a duty to take Jane to the airport.

These are *theoretical* arguments. They have moral content, but their conclusions offer propositions to be believed. Now compare the next two arguments:

26. I have the opportunity to cut off John's hand as punishment for stealing.

27. I'm tempted to cut off John's hand as punishment for stealing.

28. Cutting off a person's hand as punishment for stealing is cruel.

29. Cruel actions are evil.

30. So, I won't cut off John's hand.

31. I have the opportunity to take Jane to the airport.

32. I promised to take Jane to the airport.

33. I have a duty to keep my promises.

34. So, I will take Jane to the airport.

These are *practical* arguments. Once again, they have moral content, but their conclusions offer an act to forego or an act to carry out.

Both theoretical and practical reasoning are uniquely human. Chimps don't formulate propositions, or believe them to be true or false, or connect them inferentially to generate new propositions as we do in theoretical reasoning. Perhaps even more significantly, nothing suggests that chimps reason their way to actions from propositions. A chimp's actions are no doubt influenced and perhaps even caused by its perceptions, whereas, theoretical and practical reasoning require the power of conceiving (propositions) and then, in the first instance, inferring other propositions and, in the second instance, inferring actions. Both are amazing human capacities, which enrich human life immeasurably. But what could be their survival value? Are humans more likely to survive than chimps because they can reason theoretically and practically? The answer may not be obviously "No," but it is "No" just the same, and this, among other evidence, implies for some philosophers that humans are indeed not merely different in degree from the higher primates, but different in kind.[13]

---

13. See Difference in Degree and Difference in Kind, 56.

3

Epistemology

ORDINARY PEOPLE claim to know many things and their claims are usually legitimate and rational. We usually *know* our names, our sex, our occupation, and whether we are married or unmarried. Knowledge, then, seems to be part of normal human mental life. The area of philosophy concerned with knowledge is called *epistemology*, from *episteme*, a Greek word for knowledge. Epistemology also inquires into belief, truth, and the various ways in which they are related to knowledge.

BELIEF AND KNOWLEDGE

Humans have an extraordinary capacity to form beliefs. Most beliefs are temporary; for example, the belief that I am sitting down lasts only as long as I am seated. Other beliefs persist for years. My belief that I am a male will likely last my entire life. A belief, whether persistent or passing, is a "disposition to respond in certain ways when the appropriate issue arises."[1] My belief that I am a male disposes me to use the men's restroom.

A belief is true if it correctly maps the way things are. My belief that *Iowa is in the United States* is true if, and only

1. Quine and Ullian, *The Web of Belief*, 10.

if, Iowa is in the United States. Conversely, my belief that *Iowa is east of the Mississippi River* is false if, and only if, Iowa is not east of the Mississippi River. When I recognize that a belief is false, I automatically lose the disposition to respond in the way a "believer" would normally respond. Once I see that Iowa is not east of the Mississippi river, I am no longer disposed to drive east across the Mississippi when I want to get to Iowa.

What then is knowledge? It would be convenient if knowledge didn't exist. We would then only have to contend with true and false beliefs, which would be simpler. Most humans, however, claim to know many propositions, including where they live and what they ate for breakfast. So, although skeptics typically claim that humans can't know anything, few people are persuaded. Knowledge is intimately related to belief. It's incoherent for Thomas Jefferson to say "I know my name is Thomas, but I don't believe it," so, philosophers hold that knowledge is a special kind of belief.[2] Knowledge is also intimately related to truth. It's incoherent for Thomas Jefferson to say "I know my name is Thomas, but it isn't true that my name is Thomas," so, philosophers agree that no false belief can qualify as knowledge. Thus, two non-controversial aspects of knowledge are that (1) it must include a belief and (2) the belief must be true: to know I'm a male, I must believe that I'm a male and it must be true.

Some true beliefs are just lucky guesses, which indicates why a true belief is not equivalent to knowledge. My true belief (and lucky guess) that you are married is significantly different from my knowledge that I'm married. What

2. Quine and Ullian, *The Web of Belief*, 13.

property, then, must a true belief have to transform it into knowledge? Until 1963, most philosophers answered that question by saying that a belief had to be true and *justified* to qualify as knowledge. In that year, a fascinating paper was published by Edmund Gettier demonstrating that a belief could be both true and justified while still not qualifying as knowledge.[3] Since then, a great deal of work has been done by epistemologists to offer alternative theories. To date, while there continues to be general agreement that humans know some propositions, there is no generally accepted account of what properties a belief must have (in addition to truth) to qualify as knowledge.

TRUTH AND FALSEHOOD

Mechanics, physicians, accountants, and other ordinary people assume a real world exists, independent of their minds, and when a proposition correctly describes that world (viz. *Hydrogen has an atomic weight less than any other element*), then it is true. When a proposition incorrectly describes the real world (eg., *Hydrogen has an atomic weight greater than any other element*), then it is false. So, one simple definition of truth is to say that a proposition is true "if, and only if, things are as it says they are; and false if,

---

3. Edmund Gettier, "Is Justified True Belief Knowledge?" *Analysis* 23 (1963): 121–23. This article has been widely anthologized. See for example, Michael D. Roth and Leon Galis, eds., *Knowing* (New York: Random House, 1970) 35–38. For an important and enlightening account see, A. Plantinga, "Justification in the 20th Century" in *Philosophy and Phenomenological Research* Fall, 1990 Vol. L Supplement, 45–71.

and only if, things are not as it says they are."[4] Whether this definition is adequate bears further investigation.

Some meaningful propositions use vague terms (rich, tall) so one cannot say definitively whether they are true or false. How much money must one have to qualify as rich; how many inches of height must one have to qualify as tall? Some propositions are meaningless, such as, *'Twas brillig, and the slithy toves did gyre and gimble in the wabe.*[5] Meaningless propositions may be funny, clever, worth memorizing, and works of genius. Calling them meaningless doesn't denigrate them. It indicates merely that they lack a certain property we call *meaning*. One way to discern whether a proposition has meaning is to ask whether it can be translated from one language into another. The proposition just quoted is untranslatable. It can't be rendered into Japanese or Korean because it lacks any meaning to transfer. When vague and meaningless propositions are properly understood and eliminated from discussion, we can divide all others into those that are either true or false.[6] But, saying what it is for a proposition to be true may be more difficult than it initially appears to be. Before considering this problem, it will be useful to examine a few other properties of true propositions.

4. Sainsbury, "Philosophical Logic" in A. C. Grayling, ed., *Philosophy 1*, 105. Compare Aristotle's definition of truth and falsehood: "To say of what is that it is not, or of what is not that it is, is false, while to say of what is, that it is, and of what is not, that it is not, is true." *Metaphysics* (1011b26) Bk 4, 6.

5. Carroll, *Through the Looking Glass*, 15.

6. A worthwhile discussion of this and related matters can be found in Peter van Inwagen's chapter entitled "Objectivity" in his *Metaphysics*.

Necessary and Contingent

That some propositions are true and others false is simple enough. But among true propositions there is a further distinction between contingent truths and necessary truths. Consider two propositions:

(a) Chicago is a city in Illinois.

(b) Five multiplied by five is equal to twenty-five.

Statement (a) correctly describes the actual geographical location of the city of Chicago. But Chicago could have been located farther east along Lake Michigan, in which case it could have been in Indiana or Michigan (to give two other possible locations). Thus, statement (a) is called a *contingent truth*.

Now, consider what may be said about (b) that cannot be said about (a). (1) "five times five equals twenty-five" never *began* to be true; rather, it *always* has been true. (2) It will never in the future cease to be true. And, (3) there is no possible world in which it is false. So, proposition (b) is called a *necessary truth*.

Both (a) and (b) correctly describe the way the world is, so the difference between them is not in their truthfulness. But proposition (a) could have been false, whereas this is not so with proposition (b). One way to characterize the difference may be to say that proposition (a) is contingent because, by being potentially false, it has a weaker grip on truth than proposition (b).

A Priori and A Posteriori

The terms *a priori* and *a posteriori* come from Latin. Of the two, *a priori* is used by philosophers more frequently than *a posteriori* because sometimes the term *empirical* replaces *a posteriori*. The difference between these two phrases can be easily remembered if you notice that the first has within it the English word *prior* and the second has within it the English word *posterior*.

Begin with the second phrase. We can know some things to be the case only after (posterior to) an investigation of the way the world actually is. I can know that a tyrant possesses weapons of mass destruction, only after investigating and finding the weapons in his possession. So, my knowledge that a tyrant possesses weapons of mass destruction is *posterior* to, or *dependent on*, an empirical investigation. Philosophers refer to any proposition like *The tyrant possessed weapons of mass destruction* as *a posteriori*.

Can I know that some things are the case without investigating the way the world actually is? Such propositions would be known to be the case *prior to*, or *independent of*, empirical investigation. Suppose someone asserted that *Any tyrant who used weapons of mass destruction possessed them*. It's impossible to use something without possessing it. Therefore, I could know the proposition to be true prior to investigating whether there were any tyrants, any weapons of mass destruction, and any tyrants who possessed the weapons. Philosophers refer to any such propositions as *a priori*.

Analytic and Synthetic

The proposition *Roses have thorns* correctly describes a feature of the world, so it is true. But we can easily imagine a rose without thorns, so when we say of roses that they have thorns, we are taking two unrelated concepts, *rose* and *thorn*, and putting them together. In so doing, we are engaging in a synthesis and philosophers naturally call statements of this type *synthetic*.

Compare now two other statements: *Roses are roses* and *Roses are flowers*. Both of these statements are also true, but for a different reason. The meaning of the words makes them true. In the first instance, the concept of rose is *identical* with the concept of rose and in the second, the concept of rose *includes* the concept of flower. These assertions become apparent when we analyze the concepts of *rose* and *flower*. So philosophers call propositions of this type *analytic*.

The distinction between analytic and synthetic propositions is associated with Kant.[7] But the concept of analyticity was discussed by philosophers long before Kant.[8] More

---

7. Kant, *Critique of Pure Reason*, 48. Kant writes: "Either the predicate B belongs to the subject A, as something which is (covertly) contained in this concept A; or B lies outside the concept A, although it does indeed stand in connection with it. In the one case I entitle the judgment analytic, in the other synthetic."

8. I have taken my examples of analytic statements from John Locke who died one hundred years before Kant. See John Locke, *An Essay Concerning Human Understanding,* 306–307. For an excellent discussion of *analyticity* see Katz, "Analyticity," 11–17.

significantly, the distinction itself was powerfully challenged, clarified, and defended in the 20th century.[9]

The Pragmatic Theory of Truth

We often expect *true* beliefs to provide results that are successful, desirable, or work out for us. This powerful intuition lies behind the pragmatic theory of truth. I believe *the fastest way to drive from Dubuque, IA to Rockford, IL is by following Route 20*. If true, following Route 20 should actually enable me to arrive in Rockford after leaving Dubuque faster than any other highway.

The pragmatic theory, associated with American philosopher and psychologist William James, has much in its favor.[10] It would be confusing and dangerous if true beliefs regularly produced unsuccessful results. The issue, then, is not whether the pragmatic theory is correct, but whether it is complete. Some beliefs are incorrigible, which means that a person can't be wrong about them. At times I hold the belief that *I am in pain* and it is pretty clear that I can't be mistaken about being in pain. But what "successful result" would demonstrate the truth of this belief? For incorrigible beliefs and probably many others, the pragmatic theory is neither a necessary nor sufficient criterion of truth.[11]

---

9. On this see the challenge by Quine, "Two Dogmas of Empiricism" in *From a Logical Point of View*, 20–46 and the response by H. P. Grice and P. F. Strawson, "In Defense of a Dogma" in Ammerman, ed., *Classics of Analytic Philosophy*, 340–52.

10. James, *The Meaning of Truth*.

11. See Necessary and Sufficient, 16.

The Coherence Theory of Truth

I frequently believe *there are other people in the room with me*. If this belief is true, other propositions must also be true: *there is a room; I am in the room; other people exist; other people are in the room*, and so on. The coherence theory holds that if a belief is true, it coheres with a harmonious system of beliefs.[12] This seems entirely correct. How could a belief be true if it were inconsistent with such a harmonious system?

But therein lies a problem. The coherence theory implies that determining a belief's truth requires verifying its coherence with a harmonious system. Truth then becomes identified with verifiability.[13] By this criterion, the truth of the belief, *there are other people in the room with me*, can only be determined if someone can verify its coherence with the harmonious system. But suppose no one can. Does that imply the belief is false? Surely not. Inability to verify coherence doesn't imply falsehood.[14] There are plenty of true beliefs that can't be verified to cohere with a harmonious system including the true belief that *there are true beliefs that can't be verified to cohere with a harmonious system*. So,

12. F. H. Bradley, *Appearance and Reality*, 321–23.

13. Horwich, "truth, theories of" in Jonathan Dancy and Ernest Sosa, eds., *A Companion to Epistemology*.

14. Consider this from John Polkinghorne. "Kamerlingh Onnes discovered the totally unsuspected property of superconductivity in 1911. More than fifty years elapsed before it was explained. It could not have been understood in 1911, since it is an intrinsically quantum mechanical phenomenon and modern quantum theory was then unknown. It would have been foolish to have taken its mysterious character as a reason for denying its existence." *The Faith of a Physicist*, 27.

although coherence seems to be a necessary criterion for a belief's truth, it isn't sufficient.[15]

The Correspondence Theory of Truth

In the actual world, the state of Illinois has within its borders a city called Chicago. So, the proposition *Chicago is in Illinois* is true. According to the correspondence theory, what makes the proposition true is that it corresponds to the way the world actually is.[16]

The relation between a proposition and the world is sometimes expressed by saying propositions are true if they correspond to facts. Certain philosophers object to this by indicating various difficulties with establishing what counts as a fact. But let that pass. The correspondence theory is appealing because it expresses the way ordinary people often use the word *true*. We conclude that propositions are true when they correctly describe reality, and we conclude that propositions are false when they misstate or misrepresent reality. This is obviously the assumption behind the oath witnesses take prior to testifying in court. They promise to describe correctly the way the world was at some point in the past, or if they are an expert witness, they promise to use their professional opinion to identify correctly the cause of some event.

Most people believe there is a real world and believe that some propositions can describe it. Most philosophers are inclined to accept this as well, and that is fortunate (for

15. See Necessary and Sufficient, 16.

16. A recent defense of the correspondence theory is Fumerton, *Realism and the Correspondence Theory of Truth*. See also, Alston, *A Realist Conception of Truth*.

the philosophers). As you might expect, some philosophers deny there is a real world, and then understandably deny that any propositions correctly describe it. They say interesting things like, "[t]he aim of all such explanations is to make truth something . . . more than what our peers will, *ceteris paribus*, let us get away with saying."[17] These philosophers should be left to themselves. Some think they do harm, but mostly they should just be laughed at. Correspondence to reality may be insufficient for a comprehensive theory of truth. It may be incomplete and need to be supplemented in other ways, but it, or something like it, seems partially correct.

Perhaps the most telling criticism of the correspondence theory is that it seems to analyze truth in terms of a relation—the relation between a proposition and something that renders the proposition true. Whereas, there may be nothing that actually exists in the real world to which a true proposition is related. Consider the case of what philosophers call "negative existentials"—*slithy toves don't exist*, or *unicorns never bred in North America*. These propositions are certainly true, but to what do they correspond? As Trenton Merricks writes, ". . . there is no existing thing that is what *that hobbits do not exist* is about (in any good sense of 'about')"[18] Merricks may be correct about this, but if he is mistaken, it would be because negative existentials and subjunctive conditionals are about the real world and are true because they correctly describe that real world. Negative

17. Rorty, *Mirror of Nature*, 176.

18. Merricks, *Truth and Ontology*, 174. Or, to use another of his examples, " . . . it is false that there exists something that is what *that there might have been a dozen more fundamental particles* is about."

existentials correctly describe what the real world *lacks* and subjunctive conditionals correctly describe what is metaphysically *possible* but not *actualized* in the real world. In both cases, it seems legitimate to say that such propositions are related to the real world as correct descriptions, but this may be mistaken as the Realist Theory claims.[19]

The Realist Theory of Truth

Aristotle wrote one of the most famous definitions of truth. "To say of what is that it is not, or of what is not that it is, is false, while to say of what is, that it is, and of what is not, that it is not, is true."[20] The realist theory says that Aristotle's definition gestures at a "series of biconditionals." That *slithy toves do not exist* is true if and only if slithy toves do not exist; that *unicorns never bred in North America* is true if and only if unicorns never bred in North America; that *cows moo* is true if and only if cows moo; and that *Pegasus can fly* is true if and only if Pegasus can fly. This series of biconditionals is what is meant by *realism about truth*.[21]

Although many things recommend this theory, it is important to understand right off that proponents of the realist theory deny that it implies the correspondence theory. A Realist insists that the proposition *slithy toves do not exist* is true if and only if slithy toves do not exist. They deny, however, that *slithy toves do not exist* is about some positively existing entity. Consequently, they deny that be-

19. My thanks to Josh Hickok and David Redmond for encouraging me to think further about this.

20. Aristotle, *Metaphysics* (1011b26) Bk 4, 6.

21. Merricks, *Truth and Ontology*, 175.

ing appropriately related to some entity is what it means to assert that *slithy toves do not exist* is true.[22] Furthermore, say the realists, the correspondence theory does insist on this. A proponent of the correspondence theory might reply that the proponent of the realist theory has given a correct description of the correspondence theory, but is mistaken in claiming that the proposition *slithy toves do not exist* is not about anything. On the contrary, it is "about" the real world. Everyone understands the proposition *slithy toves do not exist* means that (in the real world) *slithy toves do not exist*. Of course, *slithy toves* exist in any number of possible worlds, but a correct description of the real world must affirm their absence here. In this way, it does not seem mistaken to think that *slithy toves do not exist* is about the real world.

In any case, let us accept the realists' insistence that their theory is not the correspondence theory. The central claim of the realist theory may be stated *negatively* as "some truths are not true in virtue of how they are related to any existing entity or entities."[23] Or, it may be stated as the claim "*being true* is not a relation between a truth and some entity."[24] The theory may be stated *positively* as the claim that *being true* is primitive in the sense of being an indefinable concept. It can't be broken down into something more basic. Other such primitive properties are *identity*, as in *I am identical with myself*, and *existence*, as in *I did not ex-*

---

22. Ibid., 176.
23. Ibid., 181.
24. Ibid., 182.

ist in 1940.[25] Primitive properties are to epistemology what quarks are to matter—the most basic constituents.

The ancient lineage of the realist theory, if indeed Aristotle can be seen as an early proponent, recommends it for strong consideration as a promising comprehensive theory. The correspondence theory remains its main competition. If the correspondence theory fails because *being true* is not a relation between truth and some entity, or if the correspondence theory is incomplete because it can account for the truth of some, but not all propositions, then the realist theory may be the best alternative.

RATIONALISM AND EMPIRICISM

The divide between rationalism and empiricism cuts through all of western philosophy. Plato (427–347 BC) was a rationalist and Aristotle (384–322 BC) an empiricist. A rationalist holds that *some knowledge* does not come from experience. A common, though misleading, way of expressing this is to say that humans have innate knowledge. An empiricist holds that *all knowledge* comes from experience. A common, and again misleading way of expressing this, is to say humans have nothing in their minds that was not in their senses first. Unless one grasps the distinction between rationalism and empiricism, the history of western philosophy will be incomprehensible.

Rationalists do not value the power of reason more or employ logic more often than empiricists. Rather, the terms *rationalist* and *empiricist* are simply traditional names assigned to these disparate views about the sources of hu-

---

25. Ibid., 186.

man knowledge. The term *rationalist* particularly has the potential to cause mischief because some non-philosophers use it as a term of derision to describe those with whom they disagree. In western philosophy, however, it is simply a descriptive term without negative connotations.

In addition to being able to assign the correct label to Plato (rationalist) and Aristotle (empiricist), any student of philosophy will need to learn how these views worked themselves out in modern philosophy. Descartes (1596–1650), the father of modern philosophy, was a rationalist, as was Leibniz (1646–1716) and Spinoza (1632–1677). Locke (1632–1704) began the empiricist response, followed by Berkeley (1685–1753) and Hume (1711–1776). Kant (1724–1804), who began as a rationalist, was goaded by Hume to attempt to articulate a rationalist-empiricism in his *Critique of Pure Reason*. Very little in post-modern philosophy can be understood without a basic grasp of the rationalist/empiricist distinction and Kant's attempt to unite the two.

REALISM AND ANTI-REALISM[26]

Mt. Kilimanjaro in Tanzania is taller than Gray's Peak in Colorado. This proposition describes the way things are in the real world. If today, by some tragedy, all human life were destroyed without affecting the earth's geography, the

---

26. Compare Realism and Idealism, 41f. It is important to understand the difference between Realism and Anti-Realism as compared with the distinction between realism and idealism. Some philosophers such as Peter van Inwagen capitalize one set of terms and leave the other in lowercase letters to highlight the difference. See, van Inwagen's chapter "Objectivity" in *Metaphysics*.

proposition would remain true. Because humans have discovered, and not invented, the heights of Mt. Kilimanjaro and Gray's Peak, the proposition is *objectively* true. This is the Realist view and can be broken down further: (a) Mt. Kilimanjaro and Gray's Peak exist in the real world; (b) their existence in no way depends on the human mind, its concepts, experience, or knowledge; and (c) the properties of these mountains (their height, for example) is also independent of the human mind, as is the relation between the two (taller than/shorter than).

Since most philosophers (fortunately) have been and are Realists, it is difficult to find an articulation of anti-Realism that is both sympathetic and clear.[27] Probably the best procedure is to consider anti-Realism with respect to one particular area of human knowledge where it can be presented persuasively. Consider mathematics. The mathematical anti-Realist would argue that: (a) the numbers nine and seven do not exist in the real world; (b) they are human mental constructs; and (c) the properties of these numbers (nine is greater than seven; seven is prime and nine is not) are also dependent on the human mind, because numbers have been invented by humans, not discovered by them. Even if you think that each of these mathematical anti-Realist contentions is false (as I do), it is clear that they are plausible. Further, and more importantly, it should also be evident that you can be a Realist in one area and an anti-

27. But consider Nelson Goodman who says: "What there is consists of what we make" and "everything including individuals is an artifact." *Of Mind and Other Matters*, 29. Plantinga calls this "creative anti-realism" as compared with "existential anti-realism." For a thorough discussion, see his "How to Be an Anti-Realist." See also, Wolterstorff, "Are Concept-Users World Makers?"

Realist in another. There is nothing inconsistent about being a Realist with respect to mountains and an anti-Realist with respect to numbers.

The fountainhead of modern anti-Realism is probably Kant. I say *probably* because there are plenty of disagreements among Kantians and Kant scholars. But everyone agrees that Kant was an anti-Realist about space and time.[28] Today, most cosmologists would likely hold that space and time are objectively real, but Kant had interesting reasons for his opinion, even if in the end he was mistaken. Principally, Kant wanted to avoid the skepticism of Hume and sought to do this by asserting that the human mind imposed order on the external world rather than assuming that the external world imposed concepts (like space and time) on the human mind.

---

28. Kant, *Critique of Pure Reason*, 67–82. Compare also the very helpful explanation of Kant's view on this subject in "Space, Time and Mathematics," chapter 2 of Korner's *Kant*, 33–42.

4

Metaphysics

AMERICAN PHILOSOPHER, W. V. O. Quine (1908–2000), began a famous paper by asking "What is there?" to which he answered "Everything."[1] Quine said everyone accepts this answer, which no doubt we do. But it doesn't get us very far. Metaphysics attempts to move things along. If we take "What is there?" as a scientific question, it can only be answered by observation. But if we take it as a philosophical question, it can only be answered by thinking.[2] Metaphysics is the part of philosophy which uses thinking to investigate ultimate reality.

By observation we can describe various human acts. Are any of these acts significantly free? Only by thinking can we hope to discover an answer. Whether ultimate reality includes human freewill is a metaphysical issue. Similarly, observation shows that humans have brains. Do we also have minds? If not, what could explain immaterial things like beliefs, intentions, or consciousness? Whether ultimate reality includes minds is a metaphysical question as well. Again, observation seems to tell us that every event has a cause. Is causation an objective part of ultimate reality or,

---

1. Quine, "On What There Is." In *From a Logical Point of View*, 1.
2. See Science and Philosophy, 2.

as Kant thought, something that humans impose on reality? Finally, is there a necessary being (God?), or is all existence contingent? Observing the world will not provide the answer; only thinking can. So, that too is a metaphysical issue.

The term *metaphysics* was first used to designate Aristotle's writings that were placed *after* his writings on physics and the word just meant "after physics." But since Aristotle's work entitled *Metaphysics* deals with the issue of *being*, which is another way of talking about ultimate reality, the name and subject matter were married.

UNIVERSAL AND PARTICULAR

I own two dogs. Each dog is obviously a *particular* dog. Do these dogs have anything in common? Maybe each particular dog possesses something that unites it with all dogs and sets dogs off from other living things. Let us call this *dogness*.[3] Is there really such a thing? If so, philosophers would call the property of dogness a *universal* because nothing can be a dog without possessing dogness and any animal that qualifies as a dog universally possesses that property.

Another way to think about this is to consider colors. Suppose I ask to see red. You might point out a red sweater or cap. Now suppose I reply that I want to see red itself, not a red sweater or cap. If you see the difficulty, you understand the difference between *particular* red things and the *universal* called *red*, or *redness*.

No one worth listening to denies the existence of particulars, but in the history of philosophy there have been interesting disagreements about the actual existence of

3. See Existence and Essence, 46.

universals.⁴ Plato (427–347 BC) is sometimes called an *extreme realist* because he believed universals were real things, existing in some kind of heavenly realm. Aristotle (384–322 BC) is sometimes called a *realist* because he believed universals were real, but existed only in particulars, i.e., red actually exists, but only in red sweaters, caps, etc. William of Ockham (AD 1285–1347), is called a *nominalist* because he denied the reality of universals, arguing instead that they were merely names. This is the source of the famous principle called *Ockham's razor* (or Occam's razor), which asserts that we should not multiply entities unnecessarily and that simplicity is best. Ockham believed that universals were unnecessary entities and that their asserted existence was an egregious philosophical error.

SUBSTANCE AND PROPERTY

Early in our lives, we learn to ask the question "What is that?" The answer we expect is usually some kind of thing: "that's a man" or "that's a horse." This is what Aristotle means by *a substance*. In his book *Categories*, he said that we can describe things in ten different ways: substance (man, horse), quantity (two hundred pounds), quality (white/brown), relative (larger/smaller), where (in Iowa), when (today), being in a position (standing), having (shoes, pants), acting on (shaving), and being affected (being shaved).⁵

---

4. See especially, Marilyn M. Adams, "Universals in the early fourteenth century" in Kretzmann et al., eds., *The Cambridge History of Later Medieval Philosophy,* 411–439. See also Crane, "Universals" in Grayling, ed. *Philosophy* 1, 204ff.

5. Aristotle, *Complete Works*, edited by J. Barnes, 4.

Of these ten, Aristotle said that *substance* was prior to the others in three ways. (i) A substance such as a horse is, in some sense, an independent unity. Being a horse implies that it has some quality, such as being brown. But the reverse is not the case; neither the quality of being brown nor the quantity of weighing two hundred pounds is an independent unity. (ii) When we try to define any other category, we find ourselves including the underlying substance in our definition. Understanding what it means to be *in a position* such as "standing" requires grasping that *a horse* has legs and when those legs are in a certain position, the horse is standing. (iii) When we want to know the answer to the question "What is it?" simply being told that "today it is standing up in Iowa with shoes on" doesn't give us the answer. Any number of substances could fit that description. We might know something about a substance if we know when and where it is in a certain position, but we know it much better when we know what substance it is.[6]

A *substance*, then, is the subject of properties in the sense that it can be said to *have* properties. A watch and shirt are items of personal property that I *have*. In a similar (though not identical) way, I *have* the property of being male and weighing a certain number of pounds. Any individual human will have innumerable properties, some of which are more important than others. Some properties are so important that without them a human would not be a human. For example, it seems impossible for me to be a human without being an animal. Philosophers call these *essential properties*. Other properties are far less important, and an individual human could gain or lose them with little

6. See David Ross' discussion of substance in *Aristotle*, 171–72.

effect. For example, I could have the property of being in Iowa one day and being in Illinois the next. Philosophers call these *accidental properties*.[7]

Most philosophers agree that properties exist, but not all agree that substances do. David Hume denied the existence of substances. In his *A Treatise of Human Nature* he said "We have no idea of substance distinct from that of a collection of particular qualities."[8] The idea seems to be that a human is not some independent unity, but just the sum total of all his or her properties. This, of course, is an interesting proposal and we might ask Hume this question: how can a bunch of properties stick together if they aren't the properties of a single substance?[9]

REALISM AND IDEALISM[10]

I exist and the desk in front of me exists. The desk is visually perceived by me; I am not perceived by the desk. Realists hold that "to *exist* is one thing, and to be *perceived* is another."[11] The "realist view" conforms to common sense;

7. See Essential and Accidental, 48.

8. I.i.,16.

9. On this and many other issues related to substance, see Wiggins, "Substance," in Grayling, ed. *Philosophy* 1, 214ff.

10. Compare Realism and Anti-Realism, 34f. It is important to understand the difference between the Realism/Anti-Realism distinction and the realism/idealism distinction. Following Peter van Inwagen, I am capitalizing one set of terms and leaving the other in lowercase letters. See, van Inwagen's chapter "Objectivity" in *Metaphysics*.

11. This is how Hylas (the realist) puts it in his dialogue with Philonous (the idealist) in George Berkeley's, *Three Dialogues Between Hylas and Philonous*, 14.

but that doesn't make it true. Idealists hold that to *exist* is just the same thing as to be *perceived*. Beginning with George Berkeley, various philosophers have been persuaded of some form of idealism.[12] If Berkeley (pronounced Bar-clay) is correct, two things follow: (i) the world consists of minds and mental ideas; and (ii) what philosophers call "material substance" does not exist.[13]

Both (i) and (ii) seem so far-fetched that most nonphilosophers think idealists are not serious, or think they can be easily refuted. Neither is the case. Suppose a realist asserts that diamonds exist and are made of a material substance called carbon. An idealist would respond by saying she is certain diamonds exist and are made of carbon, but carbon is not and could not be a material substance. Carbon is real enough, but what exactly is it? When I examine a diamond, I *perceive* something hard, so I may safely conclude that whatever else carbon is, it can't be less than hardness. Now suppose I make a list of everything about carbon that could be perceived: its weight, its extension in space, its taste and smell, the sound it makes when dropped on the floor, and any other perceivable property. The idealist holds that carbon is just all of those properties and nothing else. Notice that "material substance" is not on the list. According to the idealist, carbon is nothing more, nor less, than the

12. Idealism is more than one doctrine. The original idealism of George Berkeley is sometimes called *subjective idealism*; Kant's philosophy is sometimes called *transcendental idealism*; and the post-Kantian philosophy of Hegel is sometimes called *objective* or *absolute idealism*. There are important differences between them, but Berkeley's idealism is the fountainhead.

13. See Substance and Property, 39f, and see Wiggins, "Substance," in Grayling, ed. *Philosophy* 1, 214ff.

complete set of its perceivable properties, not the complete set of its perceivable properties plus something else that no one has ever perceived called "material substance."

The idealist, however, must add one more claim, and on this everything hinges: *a perceivable property cannot exist unperceived*. This has led to the famous question "if a tree falls in the woods and no one is there to hear it, does it make a sound?" Berkeley had a fascinating answer. He said, in effect, that of course it makes a sound because God is always there to hear it. As one recent philosopher put it, "Berkeley was unique among idealists in being entirely honest about what he is trying to say."[14] He was convinced that his idealism proved God's existence. Here is what he said: "sensible things do really exist [the hardness of carbon, for example]; and if they really exist, they are necessarily perceived by an infinite mind: therefore there is an infinite mind, or God."[15]

Thomas Reid (1710–1796) said that if you grant Berkeley his starting point, his system is impregnable.

> No demonstration can be more evident than his reasoning from it. Whatever is perceived is an idea, and an idea can only exist in a mind. It has no existence when it is not perceived; nor can there be anything like an idea, but an idea . . .[16]

If Berkeley is correct, all the objects of my own knowledge (trees, grass, cars, houses) must be ideas in my own mind. But realists stubbornly insist that this is mistaken.

14. Scruton, *Modern Philosophy*, 24.
15. Berkeley, *Three Dialogues*, 56.
16. Reid, *Essays on the Intellectual Powers of Man*, 142.

Reid wrote that in his youth he was firmly persuaded that Berkeley was correct until he asked himself "What evidence have I for this doctrine, that all the objects of my knowledge are ideas in my own mind?" And he answered that "From that time to the present I have been candidly and impartially, as I think, seeking for the evidence of this principle, but can find none, excepting the authority of philosophers."[17] Realism is not self-evidently correct any more than idealism is self-evidently mistaken. The issue is just this: is there a world that exists regardless of whether there are minds, human or divine, to perceive it? To put it slightly differently, if there were no minds presently perceiving the world, would there still be a world? The realist answers *yes* and the idealist answers *no*.[18]

BODY AND MIND

No one doubts that humans have bodies. The question is whether humans *are* bodies. Are you anything other than your body? The human body includes the brain, an amazing and intricate physical organ. When philosophers speak of the human *mind*, they do not mean the brain. They mean something non-physical, not reducible to chemistry, electromagnetism, and neurobiology.

The two most important influences on western thought, Greek philosophy and Christianity, both assert that humans are a composite of the physical and non-physical. The word *soul* was traditionally used to designate the non-

17. Ibid.

18. A recent defense of a modified form of idealism is Adams, "Idealism Vindicated."

physical part. The modern philosophical concept of mind differs from the Platonic concept of soul; but some modern philosophers use soul interchangeably with mind.[19] The important thing is to understand that modern philosophers take a wide variety of interesting positions regarding the reality (or unreality) of mind.

At one extreme are the *dualists* for whom physical properties and mental properties are distinct, but equally real. The great and ongoing problem for dualists is how something non-physical (the mind) can affect and be affected by something physical (the body). This is one of the problems that vexed Descartes, who was the original modern dualist. At the other extreme are the *eliminativists* for whom mental properties are unreal and should be eliminated. The great and ongoing problem for eliminativists is how such things as beliefs, intentions, and purposes (all arguably mental entities) can be explained by and reduced to neurobiology. Since it is difficult to deny that humans have beliefs, and since beliefs have non-physical properties like truth and falsehood (what can it possibly mean to say that a chemical or electrical impulse is true or false?), the prospect of eliminating the mental is very dim. Between these two extremes lie fascinating philosophical puzzles, including the problem of freewill. If humans have only brains, which like all other material things are subject to the laws of physics, how could we have freewill? More crucially, without some kind of significant liberty of our wills, can we rightly be held morally responsible for our actions?

---

19. See, for instance, Swinburne, *The Evolution of the Soul*.

EXISTENCE AND ESSENCE

One difference between me and Santa Claus is that I exist and Santa doesn't.[20] Medieval philosophers would have said that I have *being* (*esse*) and Santa Claus lacks *being*.[21] One difference between me and my dog is that I'm a member of the species *homo sapiens* and my dog is a member of the species *canis familiaris*. Medieval philosophers would have said that I have one kind of essence or nature (*essentia*) and my dog has another. When we put these concepts together, we can say that any finite being is composed of *what it is* (its essence or nature) and *that it is* (its existence or being). Together, these concepts provide one way to conceive of reality, and, since the Middle Ages, the distinction has had a long and important history in western philosophy.[22]

Let us suppose with the medieval philosophers that my dog and I are composites of *being* and *essence*. In my case, a human essence (nature) is actualized (given existence or being), and in my dog's case, a canine essence is actualized. As with many things in philosophy, this way of looking at reality is simultaneously interesting and controversial. Are there really natures or essences—dogness, catness, humanness?

If there is such a thing as humanness, it is a set of necessary properties that all humans possess? A necessary prop-

20. This is true even if the legend of Santa Claus is based loosely on the historical person St. Nicholas, the 4th century Bishop of Myra, Lucia and patron saint of Russia.

21. In Latin *esse* equals being.

22. For part of this history, see Wippel, "Essence and Existence" in Kretzmann et al., eds., *Cambridge History of Later Medieval Philosophy*, 385–410.

erty is the same as an essential property—something which, if you were to lose, you would not merely be different from what you are, you would cease to exist. So, for example, it seems to make sense to say that a human must be an animal. No human is a number, mineral, or plant. Similarly, it seems that a human must be a mammal. No human is a marsupial or reptile. Other necessary or essential human properties might be the potential for self-consciousness and freedom of the will. If you put all necessary (essential) human properties together, you have human essence or nature.

To medieval philosophers, it was evident that humans are not the causes of their own existence. Existence is not one of the necessary properties that make up human nature (or canine or feline nature either). The conclusion inferred from this observation was that "to the extent that every created being is not the cause of its own existence, [medieval philosophers] all agreed that there is a real distinction between the essence of a being as known to the mind of God and the same essence turned by the creative power of God into an actually existing being."[23] But doesn't this imply that there are essences without existence? And if so, how could that be? Historians of medieval philosophy assure us that the distinction does not have that implication; rather the distinction "simply means that there is a feature of a thing, namely its essence, which can be understood without knowing whether such an essence has being in the universe of things."[24]

A great deal more was said about this distinction during the Middle Ages. Today, philosophers continue to use these concepts and think about their relation to each other.

23. Gilson, *History of Christian Philosophy*, 421.
24. Weinberg, *Medieval Philosophy*, 185.

In the twentieth century, a philosophical view known as existentialism was popular among many European philosophers. According to French philosopher Jean Paul Sartre (1905–1980), this is the view that humans are radically free, and therefore their *existence* precedes their *essence*, i.e., what I am is a consequence of the choices I make, not of some archetypal essence known to the mind of God. Other philosophers have explored whether in addition to *kind essences* (dogness, catness, humanness) there might also be *individual essences*, a set of essential properties that is unique to you or unique to me and by which we can be identified in any possible world in which we exist, including the real world.[25]

Essential and Accidental

The world seems to be composed of many distinct objects. Rather than arguing for this view, suppose for the moment that it accurately describes the way the world is: each star, planet, tomato, and seed is an object distinct from the others, and has a certain set of properties.[26] Properties are best understood by examples. The planet on which we live called Earth has the following properties: spherical, populated, in motion around the sun, and capable of supporting sentient life. Many philosophers have held that the set of properties

---

25. See especially Saul A. Kripke, *Naming and Necessity*, 42ff, and Plantinga, "De Essentia" in *Essays in the Metaphysics of Modality*, 139.

26. This view of the world has been called by one philosopher the "common western metaphysic," by which he means, "the core of metaphysical belief that is common to most of the views of the World that are held by ordinary, unreflective people in Europe and the English-speaking countries." Peter van Inwagen, *Metaphysics*, 20, 21.

possessed by each object can be divided into two categories: *essential* properties and *accidental* properties.[27]

My weight and the number of hairs on my head are *accidental* properties, not because I possess them by chance, but because when they change I continue to exist as the same person I have always been. My weight fluctuates, and each year I (probably) have fewer hairs. Essential properties are different in an interesting and important way. It appears evident to me that I have the property of being free in some significant sense.[28] I make choices for which I am responsible, choices that are genuinely blameworthy or praiseworthy. Suppose again that this accurately describes me. If I possess this property essentially, I can't lose it and continue to exist. To lose it is the same thing as ceasing to exist.

It may be easier to understand this distinction by focusing on divine properties. Omniscience (maximal knowledge), omnipotence (maximal power) and omnibenevolence (maximal moral goodness) are divine properties. Theists hold that these are among the essential properties possessed by God. If God were to fail to have maximal power, God would not limp along as an omniscient, omnibenevolent, but weak God. No such being as God would exist. Many philosophers hold that all of God's properties are essential, i.e., God has no accidental properties at all. But recently some philosophers have suggested reasons to doubt that this is the case. Under any circumstances, the distinction between essential and accidental properties continues to be a matter of interest to contemporary philosophers.

---

27. In some older books, properties are sometimes called attributes, as in "the attributes of God."

28. See Freewill and Determinism, 50.

FREE WILL AND DETERMINISM

Suppose I give a large sum of money to feed starving children. The gift has good consequences, but should I be praised for making the gift? That depends in part on whether I have acted freely. Most of us believe that we are responsible only when we have acted freely. If my gift was caused (determined) by a threat (an external compulsion), I should not be praised. About this, there is almost universal agreement. But this agreement sets the stage for profound and interesting disagreements.

The first area of disagreement regards the definition of freedom or liberty. Medieval philosophers differentiated between two kinds of liberty, the *liberty of spontaneity* and the *liberty of indifference*.[29] Those who espoused the liberty of spontaneity asserted that you are responsible for your actions if, and only if, *you do what you want to do*. Those who espoused the liberty of indifference asserted that you are responsible for your actions if, and only if, *you could have refrained*. In the first case, responsibility hinges on intent; in the second case, it hinges on the power to do otherwise. This is an important difference because I can intend to do something without having the power to do otherwise. Suppose I see a young boy trapped in a burning building and intentionally rescue him. Later when interviewed about my heroism, I might say (truthfully) that I could not have refrained from rescuing him. If liberty of spontaneity is sufficient for responsibility, then I should still be praised

---

29. See especially the two chapters entitled "Foreknowledge and Indeterminism" and "Foreknowledge and Determinism" in Kenny, *The God of the Philosophers*.

Metaphysics 51

for rescuing him. This seems at least plausible. However, today many philosophers consider liberty of spontaneity to be inferior to liberty of indifference and consequently refer to the latter as "significant freedom."[30]

Whichever definition of freewill we adopt, two kinds of determinism seem to eliminate it and undermine responsibility. Peter van Inwagen defines determinism as the thesis that "given the past and the laws of nature, there is only one possible future."[31] It's very hard to see how, if there is only one possible future, anyone could make a free choice, particularly if the future is determined by the past and the laws of nature. This would mean that, despite the obvious fact that humans deliberate about their future actions (what to have for breakfast, where to go to college, whom to marry), the outcome of the deliberation is determined by the past and the laws of nature. If this seems false, then asserting that humans have freewill entails that (i) there is more than one possible future and (ii) what the future will be is not determined by the past and the laws of nature.

Another fascinating kind of determinism involves God's knowledge.[32] Suppose God existed in 1949 (prior to my birth) and knew then that I would be typing these words today. It is impossible for anyone, including God, to know what is false.[33] If it were within my power to refrain from typing these words today, it would be within my power to bring it about that God did not know in 1949 that I would

30. Plantinga, *God, Freedom, and Evil*, 30.

31. van Inwagen, *An Essay on Free Will*, 65.

32. This argument was developed by Pike in his article "Divine Omniscience and Voluntary Action."

33. See Belief and Knowledge, 20f.

be typing these words today. But surely this is impossible for three reasons. (i) I can't change the past. (ii) I can't bring it about that God doesn't know something. And (iii) I can't bring it about that God doesn't exist. But, if God knew in 1949 that I would be typing these words, surely I don't have the power to refrain from typing them, however much I might think that I do. If freewill requires only that I intend to type the words (liberty of spontaneity), there is no problem. I am acting freely despite my inability to refrain and I'm responsible. But, if freewill requires the power to refrain (liberty of indifference), then I'm not acting freely and I'm not responsible.[34]

Compatibilism and Incompatibilism

Suppose that you have freewill—either you are able to act intentionally (liberty of spontaneity) or in some cases you have the power to refrain or do otherwise (liberty of indifference). Is either kind of freedom compatible with determinism? Some philosophers say yes and are, naturally enough, called *compatibilists*. Others say no and are called *incompatibilists*.[35]

---

34. Boethius had a fascinating solution to this dilemma. See, Boethius, *The Consolation of Philosophy,* Book V, section VI. He claimed that God is timeless, and as such did not exist in 1949, nor in any other year. God's existence cannot be located in time any more than his existence can be located in space. God knows that I am typing these words, but he knows it timelessly, which eliminates any problem with my freewill. For an excellent brief discussion see Brian Leftow, "Eternity" in Philip L. Quinn and Charles Taliaferro, *A Companion to Philosophy of Religion*, 257–63.

35. See the chapter entitled "Compatibilism and Incompatibilism" in Honderich, *How Free Are You?*

Many philosophers (the incompatibilists) believe that liberty of indifference is necessary for responsibility and believe further that there is genuinely more than one possible future. Conversely, many scientists, though not all, are materialists—they believe that all events can be explained by the laws of biology, chemistry, and, ultimately, physics. For them, determinism is true—"given the past and the laws of nature, there is only one possible future."[36] They might be classed as compatibilists, but only if they also believe that humans have some kind of freewill, which many of them simply deny.

There seems, then, to be three views that are actually held. (i) Some people are determinists. These are often scientists who espouse materialism. They deny that humans have freewill in any sense and, to be consistent, also deny that humans are responsible for any of their actions. (ii) Many eminent philosophers of the past have been compatibilists. They have usually adopted the view that freewill is best understood as the liberty of spontaneity and, given that assumption, have also asserted that determinism and freewill are compatible. You and I are responsible for our actions so long as we have done what we intended to do. (iii) Today, incompatibilism is probably the dominant view among analytic philosophers.[37] It seems to them that "significant freedom" requires the power to refrain or the power to do otherwise (liberty of indifference). You and I are only responsible for our actions if we genuinely could have acted in a way different from how we did act. This implies that our deliberations are meaningful and that there is more than one possible future.

36. Peter van Inwagen, *An Essay on Free Will*, 65.
37. See Analytic Philosophy and Continental Philosophy, 78f.

FOUR ARISTOTELIAN CAUSES

Aristotle noticed that many things come into being and then perish. Our curiosity inclines us to ask why such changes take place, and Aristotle believed there were four possible answers.[38] Philosophers refer to these as the four Aristotelian causes: material, formal, efficient, and final. Aristotle himself did not use the last two terms, but he held that coming to be, perishing, and change in general, take place for four different reasons or combinations of reasons. These terms continue to be used by philosophers and others to explain many different things. They are easy to understand and remember if you focus on a simple object like a chair.

Material Cause

I'm presently sitting on a chair made of wood. No one knows what material was used to make the very first chair in history. Perhaps it was made of wood or stone. Chairs today are made of plastic, steel, and even glass. What seems certain is that if you are going to make a chair, you must use some kind of material or combination of materials. This is the *material cause* of a thing or *that from which* it is made.

Formal Cause

At some time in the ancient past there were no chairs. No one knows who made the first chair, but someone did. The person who made the first chair conceived (thought of) the

---

[38]. Aristotle discussed the four causes in four different places in his works: *Physics*, 194b20–195a3; *De Generatione et Corruptione*, 335a28–336a12; *De Partibus Animalium*, 639b12–639b21; and *Metaphysics*, 983a24–983b6.

form that today we associate with chairs. The human mind is able to see *many* chairs and draw out (abstract) from them the *one* form they all share. The formal cause of any chair is *that into which* it is made.

Efficient Cause

I don't know who made the chair I am presently sitting on, but someone did. Whoever made it is the *efficient cause* of the chair. Today, when we seek the cause of some object or event, we are usually looking for its efficient cause. Another way to put this is to say that in the question "Who caused this to come into being?" the meaning of the word "cause" is what philosophers mean by "efficient cause." So, the efficient cause of a chair is *that by which* it is made.

Final Cause

Why would anyone go to the trouble of making a chair? The obvious answer is so that someone can sit on it. The purpose or function of a chair (to be sat on) is its *final cause*. Aristotle believed that we could identify the function of various parts of our body. For example, the eye's function is to see, and the ear's function is to hear. Aristotle also seemed to conclude that because each part has a function, the whole must also have a function, and there he may have been mistaken.[39] When Darwin discovered the law of natural selection, whereby matter seems to organize itself randomly and without purpose, biologists declared that there are no *final causes* in nature. This is a fascinating claim which continues

---

39. In *Nicomachean Ethics*, 1097b30 he puts this somewhat tentatively.

to produce controversy. Many theists are willing to agree that natural selection is a law of nature, but are unwilling to agree that it eliminates *final causes*. Some atheists, on the contrary, believe that *final causes* are the mortal enemy of natural selection. In any case, a final cause is *that for which* something is made.

DIFFERENCE IN DEGREE AND DIFFERENCE IN KIND

Biologists tell us that chimpanzees are the closest animal relatives to humans. Still, pretty obviously, humans and chimps are different. How should that difference be measured? Perhaps chimps are different from us merely in *degree*. A four inch line and a twelve inch line both have the property of *length*. Because a twelve inch line has more length than a four inch line, it is *different in degree*. We may be different from chimps in a similar way. This would mean that chimps and humans have generally the same properties (intelligence, self-awareness, tool-making ability, etc.), but humans have more of some properties and (possibly) less of others.

But that may be mistaken. Perhaps humans and chimps are *different in kind*. A square possesses four right angles and two sets of parallel lines. A circle possesses no right angles, no parallel lines, and each point along the circle is equidistant from the center, a property that squares lack. So squares and circles are *different in kind*, and we may be different from chimps in a similar way. For example, we seem to have the ability to deliberate, to act freely, and to distinguish a morally right action from a morally wrong action.[40] There seems to be no hard evidence that chimps deliberate, have freewill, or can distinguish a morally right from morally wrong action, and this would mean that humans possess essential properties that chimps lack completely. Philosophers frequently use the distinction between *degree* and *kind*, and one interesting point may be that the human ability to distinguish between *degree* and *kind* itself indicates that we are *different in kind* from the higher primates.

---

40. See Right and Wrong, 60.

5

Moral Philosophy/Ethics

HUMANS ARE unique in their ability to distinguish right from wrong and good from bad. Examples are easy to imagine: feeding the hungry is right; starving the helpless is wrong; an abundant wheat harvest is good; a famine is bad. Moral philosophers examine these distinctions systematically and attempt to account for the features of actions that make them right or wrong and the characteristics of states of affairs and persons that make them good or bad. All of us keep or break promises, speak kind or cruel words, eat more or less than we should. We don't merely do these things, we think about them as well, and our thinking engages us in moral philosophy. Probably no area of philosophy is more significant and interesting than moral philosophy.

IS AND OUGHT

The proposition *"Torture is used by some governments to extract information"* states what *is the case*. The proposition *"Torture ought never to be used by any governments"* states what *ought to be the case*, but sometimes is not. The first *describes* and the second *prescribes*. Because this distinction is so important, the wise person will learn to differentiate propositions in the first class from those in the second. In this regard, it helps to see that the verbs *can* (and *can't*) are related to the verb *is* as *should* (and *shouldn't*) are related to the verb *ought*. "I shouldn't lie even to save lives" purports to *prescribe* how I ought to act; whereas, "I can't lie even to save lives" is used by some to mean the same thing, but it doesn't. Failing to differentiate between these two kinds of propositions will cause confusion, so using them interchangeably should be carefully avoided.

Learning the distinction between *is* and *ought* enables you to understand the significance of the question whether *ought* statements ever follow logically from *is* statements. David Hume famously noted the problems associated with trying to derive *ought* statements from *is* statements.[1] Because *it is the case that some men have sex with their daughters* it, fortunately, does not follow that *some men ought to have sex with their daughters*. But from the fact that *my children need clothing*, it does seem to follow that *I ought to cloth my children*. What's the difference? Many moral philosophers would say the difference lies in the unarticulated addition in the second case of two premises, namely, *I have a duty to cloth my children* and *I ought to do my duty*.[2] Seeing this also explains why no such entailment exists between the first set of statements. Not only is the statement *fathers have a duty to have sex with their daughters* false, but *fathers have a duty not to have sex with their daughters* is true.

1. David Hume, *A Treatise of Human Nature*, Bk III, sect. 1.
2. Nicholas Rescher's essay "How Wide is the Gap Between Facts and Values" will reward careful study.

RIGHT AND WRONG

Some acts are right and others are wrong. Right acts ought to be done; wrong acts ought not to be done. Cross-culturally and cross-temporally, the overwhelming majority of humans have endorsed these assertions.[3] The five major world religions, Hinduism, Buddhism, Judaism, Christianity, and Islam, all specifically teach that lying, murder, stealing, and adultery are wrong. Conversely, telling the truth, preserving life, respecting the property of others, and keeping promises are right. The universality of these prescriptions comes as a great shock to those who have taken in moral subjectivism with their mother's milk. But simple truths have a way of doing that.

Both in moral philosophy and in normal linguistic usage, right and wrong describe acts, never objects or states of affairs. Books may be good, but they are not right; hurricanes may be bad, but they are not wrong. Perhaps this reflects our intuition that, as moral properties, rightness and wrongness require intent. Acts may fulfill duties or harm others, but they are right or wrong only if they were intended.[4]

We also express moral approval or disapproval of acts by means of these terms. Some moral philosophers in the twentieth century (emotivists) argued that this was their only use. However, emotivism as a comprehensive moral theory has mercifully fallen into disfavor. It seems more

---

3. For evidence, see the appendix to C. S. Lewis' *The Abolition of Man* entitled "The Tao."

4. See Freewill and Determinism, 50.

likely that rightness and wrongness are real properties that supervene[5] on some intentional actions.

GOOD AND EVIL

One of the most famous stories in philosophy is Plato's allegory of the cave found in *The Republic*. Imagine humans in an underground cave with legs and neck bound and permitted only to look straight ahead. Behind them burns a fire; between them and the fire a road runs, on which people walk carrying statutes of animals and humans, the shadows of which can be seen on the cave's wall. One of the prisoners escapes. As he moves out of the cave, his eyes initially hurt, but when he becomes accustomed to the light, he sees reflections in water, and soon sees things themselves rather than their shadows. Finally, he sees the sun.

According to Plato, this story represents the soul's assent toward "the idea of the good."[6] Once the good is seen, "it must be concluded that this is in fact the cause of all that is right and fair in everything."[7] For Plato, the good is a uni-

---

5. The normal definition of "supervene" is this: properties of type-A supervene on properties of type-B if and only if two objects cannot differ with respect to their A-properties without also differing with respect to their B-properties. See Audi, ed., *The Cambridge Dictionary of Philosophy*, s.v. "superenience." If the color of a rose supervenes on the chemical makeup of the flower, then two roses cannot differ with respect to their color without differing with respect to their chemical makeup. In moral philosophy, it cannot be morally wrong for me to shoot you in the head intentionally, but be morally right for someone else to shoot you in the head intentionally.

6. Plato, *The Republic*, (517c), in Cooper, ed., *Plato: Complete Works*.

7. Ibid.

ty, objectively real, discoverable by humans, and the source from which all earthly things receive their "goodness."

In the *Nicomachean Ethics*, Aristotle argued that Plato erred in thinking that "the good" had only one form. "Goodness" is commonly attributed to such disparate things as minds, virtues, useful things, times, and places. So, Aristotle argued, "the good" cannot be some common or universal essence. Rather, "it is apparently one thing in one action or craft, and another thing in another."[8] Aristotle's disagreement with Plato regarding the unity of the good, did not dissuade him from claiming that the variety of "goods" were objectively real; nor did he doubt that they were discoverable by humans.

Early Christian philosophers such as Augustine (354–430) and medieval philosophers such as Aquinas (1225–1274) found much to affirm in the giants of Greek philosophy, not least of which was their affirmation of the objective reality of "the good" (in the case of Plato) and the "goods" (in the case of Aristotle). Because Christian philosophers identified "the good" with God's nature and located the source of all finite "goods" in the creative power of God, the objectivity of "goodness" was secured by tying it to God's objective existence.

Many philosophers who categorize themselves as atheists understandably reject any claim to the objectivity of goodness, preferring instead to argue for the subjectivity of values. Antony Flew, among the most articulate exponents of this view, wrote that "if two men differ about values, there is not a disagreement as to any kind of truth,

---

8. *Nicomachean Ethics*, (1097a15) Bk 1.

but a difference of taste."⁹ Further, argued Flew, "The chief ground for adopting this view is the complete impossibility of finding any arguments to prove that this or that has intrinsic value."¹⁰ If one man holds that governments ought to occasionally torture humans, and another holds that they never ought to do so, the disagreement is not over the truth or falsehood of the statement "Torture, being intrinsically evil, should always be prohibited"; it is rather that one man has a taste for torture and the other does not. To put Flew's position in a slightly different way, goodness and evil are not real properties of events or states of affairs as are properties such as *painful, pleasurable, death causing,* and *life producing.*

If goodness and evil are not real properties, then clearly there is no such thing as evil. This is the position taken by A. C. Grayling who opines that "'Evil' . . . means whatever a religion dislikes."¹¹ He then proceeds to assert that "There is no greater social evil than religion."¹² This latter assertion is equivalent to "There is no greater social *state of affairs that religions dislike* than religion," which is certainly clap-trap and illustrates one of the difficulties with the subjectivist view of good and evil.

In western philosophy, the most influential view of evil comes from Augustine who held that evil is the absence of good. Speaking of disease as a natural evil, Augustine

9. Flew, *An Introduction to Western Philosophy*, 115.

10. Ibid., 115. Flew has since become a theist, but it is unclear whether he has changed his mind about "intrinsic value." See, Flew, *There is a God.*

11. Grayling, *Life, Sex and Ideas*, 33.

12. Ibid., 34.

states that "Evil, then, is ... a privation of that good which is called health."[13] As darkness is the real absence of light, evil is the real absence of good.

NATURAL LAW

The natural law tradition began with Aristotle.[14] "What is natural," he said, "has the same validity everywhere alike, independent of its seeming so or not."[15] *Natural justice*, in Aristotle's sense, implies that some laws, duly enacted, published and enforced, are unjust if they fail to meet the universal standard of justice. In the United States, the laws enforcing racial segregation in the south during the first half of the twentieth century would be prime examples. This seems plain enough, but natural law remains the most misunderstood ancient or modern moral theory. "Verily," wrote William Frankena, "the ways of the natural law tradition are many and past all finding out!"[16]

The concept of natural law was expounded by the Roman statesman Cicero (106–43 BC)[17], incorporated into Christian philosophy by Augustine and then Aquinas,[18]

---

13. Augustine, *Enchiridion*, Chapter 3, Sec. 11.

14. Some would say natural law begins with Plato. See Buckle's brief history in "Natural Law" in Peter Singer, ed., *A Companion to Ethics*.

15. Aristotle, *Nicomachean Ethics*, Bk 2, chapter 7.

16. Frankena, "On Defining and Defending Natural Law," 203.

17. See Cicero *De Re Publica; De Legibus*, III, xxii. "True law is right reason in agreement with nature; it is of universal application, unchanging and everlasting; it summons to duty by its commands, and averts from wrongdoing by its prohibitions."

18. See Augustine, *The City of God*, II, 21 and Aquinas, *Summa*

and influenced the founding of the American republic through the work of John Locke.[19] Four common threads run through this tradition. (i) Some states of affairs are objectively beneficial (good) for humans while others are objectively harmful (bad). Benefit and harm are not matters of convention or based on common agreement; they are discoverable just as the Rocky Mountains were discovered by the Lewis and Clark Expedition. (ii) Reason dictates that which benefits humans and that which harms them. This can be put in two ways: the good for humans is governed by reason, or humans will flourish if they govern their lives by reason. (iii) Moral skepticism, the view that there are no correct answers to moral questions, is mistaken. (iv) The good for humans which is dictated by reason (the law of human nature) is "written on the heart" by God. Paul of Tarsus was the first Christian to make this point. In his letter to the Romans he wrote that non-Jews, ". . . show that the work of the law is written on their hearts, while their conscience also bears witness . . ."[20] The pre-Christian philosopher, Cicero, asserted that ". . . one eternal and unchangeable law will be valid for all nations and all times, and there will be one master and ruler, that is, God, over us all, for he is the author of this law, its promulgator, and its enforcing judge."[21]

Objectors are legion, among whom some count Thomas Hobbes (1588–1679) who asserted that "no Law can be Unjust."[22] But this is just another illustration of the

---

Theologiae, I–II QQ 90.

19. See John Locke, *Two Treatises of Government*.
20. See Romans 2:14–15.
21. *De Re Publica; De Legibus*, III, xxii.
22. Hobbes, *Leviathan*, 239.

curious difficulties and tensions that one finds within natural law theory, for, despite his apparent equation of justice and law, Hobbes distinguished good laws from bad laws. A good law, according to Hobbes, was that "which is *Needfull, for the Good of the People,* and withal *Perspicuous.*"[23] Would it not be correct then to suppose that the badness of a bad law is at least partly a consequence of its injustice?

DEONTOLOGY

Any moral philosophy which places duty above all else is a type of deontology, so named because the Greek word *deon* means duty. The most influential deontology was articulated by Immanuel Kant, who argued that all rational beings have a duty to conform their lives to a moral principle he called *the categorical imperative.* He formulated this principle in various ways, the easiest of which to understand is: always treat other humans as ends and never as means.[24]

Deontology, especially as articulated by Kant, has obvious attractions. The existence of duties seems obvious to most people, and making sense of human life without duties may well be impossible. Some duties are voluntary, such as your duty to keep a promise if you make one; some duties are involuntary, such as your duty to feed your children even if you didn't want them to be born. We routinely

---

23. Ibid.

24. Kant, *Grounding for the Metaphysics of Morals*, (430), 37. A more difficult articulation of the categorical imperative is "I should never act except in such a way that I can also will that my maxim should become a universal law." *Grounding for the Metaphysics of Morals*, (402), 14.

hold ourselves and others responsible to fulfill duties and justly condemn those who refuse.

It is highly unlikely that any adequate account of duty can be given from within an atheistic world view. The duty of a parent to feed a child confers no benefit on the parent and conforming one's life to Kant's categorical imperative may well result in a marked or even permanent loss of personal fulfillment. Certainly conforming your life to the involuntary duty to feed your children confers no *survival* benefit on you. An atheistic world, in which duties exist that require ultimate personal sacrifice, is an irrational world, a world that makes no sense.[25] If you are inclined to think that involuntary and voluntary duties actually exist, you will have a difficult time explaining their existence if you are an atheist, but an easier time explaining their existence if you are a theist.

CONSEQUENTIALISM

Actions have consequences—some good, others bad. A moral philosophy which makes consequences central must be at least partially on the right track. Utilitarianism asserts that consequences alone determine the rightness or wrongness of any action. This view was most famously expounded by John Stuart Mill (1806–1873), who wrote a series of essays published together in 1861 under the title *Utilitarianism*.[26]

---

25. On this point see the powerful and persuasive argument of Mavrodes, "Religion and the Queerness of Morality," 213–26. But see also Taylor, *Ethics, Faith, and Reason*, 84, who says " . . . the concept of moral obligation [is] unintelligible apart from the idea of God. The words remain but their meaning is gone."

26. Many editions are in print. Every anthology of readings in

In these essays, Mill defended and developed the moral philosophy of Jeremy Bentham (1748–1832), one of his father's closest friends.

According to Mill, if an action produces the greatest good for the greatest number of people, the action is morally right. Conversely, if an action produces more evil than good for the greatest number of people, it is morally wrong. This requires an important clarification. Mill does not mean an action is *morally* right if it produces the greatest amount of *moral* goodness. Such a definition would fail to enlighten us about both moral rightness and moral goodness. He means an action is morally right if it produces the greatest amount of non-moral good. Intellectual pleasure, economic prosperity, and physical health are all examples of non-moral goods.[27] It is convenient to use the phrase *human well-being* to describe the aggregate of non-moral goods.

Utilitarianism has had many capable defenders, as well as sharp critics. Its strongest recommendation is that it incorporates consequences into moral discourse—something all competent parents teach their children. Among a variety of criticisms raised against utilitarianism, probably the most powerful is the following: suppose an action such as lying produces exactly the same amount of non-moral good and non-moral evil. The utilitarian seems bound to conclude that, under such circumstances, it makes no difference whether a person lies or speaks the truth. But surely

---

moral philosophy or philosophy in general will have part or all of this work.

27. As compared with promise-keeping and truth-telling, which are moral goods.

this is false, which implies that consequences alone cannot determine the rightness or wrongness of an action.[28]

VIRTUE ETHICS

Virtues are human excellences. Aristotle asserted that some human excellences, such as justice, are moral (virtues of character) and some, such as wisdom, are intellectual (virtues of thought). The area of moral philosophy called "virtue ethics" focuses primarily on virtues of character, considering what they are and how humans acquire them.

Aristotle denied that any virtue of character could arise in a human naturally.[29] Our hearing and seeing are both natural; we don't hear or see by practicing. By contrast, a person becomes a pianist by practicing the piano. Aristotle believed that acquiring moral virtue was analogous to acquiring skill in piano playing. A person becomes just by practicing justice. Furthermore, human dispositions to act in various ways can be placed on a continuum. Suppose on one end of the continuum we place actions recognized as *cowardly* (breaking up with your girlfriend by sending her a text message rather than speaking to her in person). On the other end of the continuum we place actions recognized as *rash* (breaking up with your boyfriend when he fails a philosophy class). Between these two extremes lies *courage* (speaking honestly and in person with your boyfriend or girlfriend regarding the difficulties in your relationship). Aristotle believed all moral virtues could be plotted on a continuum between two extremes: excess (viz.

28. Frankena makes this point in *Ethics*, 41–42.
29. *Nicomachean Ethics*, Bk II, 1.

rashness) and deficiency (viz. *cowardice*).[30] Whether this is so has been challenged by some moral philosophers who have high regard for virtue, but who think that some virtues like honesty have no excess, only deficiency (in this case, dishonesty).

This ancient focus of moral philosophy fell into disrepute for several hundred years during the modern era of philosophy when morality was conceived as primarily about doing one's duty or following a principle or rule that would yield right conduct. In the late twentieth century, virtue ethics was revived and the debate now continues.[31] We may put the question like this: what is most primary in morality—the moral principle imposing on me the duty to treat all people equally, or my disposition actually to treat people equally? Or, to put the matter slightly differently, which is more important: that I treat people equally because I have a duty to do so, or that my character is so formed that I am internally disposed to treat people equally? Fortunately, we need not choose between these options. There is nothing contradictory about emphasizing both the observance of duties and the well-being produced by virtue.

DIVINE COMMAND ETHICS

Suppose certain acts are commanded and others are forbidden by God. Suppose further that God has made these commands and prohibitions sufficiently plain that most people are aware of them. Many monotheists believe this correctly describes the human moral situation. If asked why

30. *Nicomachean Ethics*, BK II, 6.
31. See most notably, MacIntyre, *After Virtue*.

lying, adultery, murder and stealing are wrong, they answer that God forbids them. If asked why truth telling, marital fidelity, protection of human life and respect for other's property are right, they answer that God commands these acts or commands acts that promote these ends.

In Judaism, God's commands and prohibitions are integral to the moral life and prescribe the form of anything that counts as a good life. God's commands and prohibitions include the Ten Commandments that are listed twice in the Pentateuch (Exodus 20 and Deuteronomy 5). One interesting way to view these commands is to see them as addressing the four major areas of human problems: wealth, sex, speech, and force.[32] The revival of philosophy of religion during the past thirty years by British and American analytic philosophers generated a renewed interest in divine command ethics. This interest and its developments have included the publication of numerous articles in scholarly journals as well as book length treatments.[33]

Euthyphro Dilemma

Four hundred years before the birth of Jesus of Nazareth, Plato recorded a conversation between Socrates and Euthyphro in which the central problem with divine command ethics was articulated.[34] Euthyphro had just charged his own father with murder for causing the death of a slave who had himself committed murder. Socrates was shocked by Euthyphro's behavior toward his own father and sought

32. Smith, *The World's Religions*, 286.

33. See especially, Quinn, "The Recent Revival of Divine Command Ethics."

34. Plato, *Euthyphro*, in Cooper, ed., *Plato: Complete Works*.

to undermine Euthyphro's annoying self-justification by asking for his definition of piety. Socrates easily showed the inadequacies of Euthyphro's definitions, and in the course of their conversation, illustrated the problem with any moral theory that appeals to God's will as the basis for judging that acts are right or wrong.

When stripped of its polytheism and placed into a monotheistic context the problem can be stated in the form of a valid constructive dilemma:

1. If acts are right (or wrong) because they are commanded (or prohibited) by God, then morality is arbitrary. And, if acts are right (or wrong) irrespective of God's commands (and prohibitions), then morality is independent of God.

2. Either acts are right (or wrong) because they are commanded (or prohibited) by God, or they are right (or wrong) irrespective of God's commands (or prohibitions).

3. Therefore, either morality is arbitrary or independent of God.

The disjunction presented in the conclusion is incompatible with any coherent theory of divine command morality. To avoid the conclusion, I must either "grasp the horns" of the dilemma, i.e., attack the first premise, or "escape through the horns," i.e., attack the second premise. In the first case, if I am a defender of divine command morality, I must show that morality is not arbitrary even if actions are right (or wrong) because they are commanded (or prohibited) by God. Robert Adams adopted this approach in his ground breaking defense of divine command ethics.³⁵ In the second case, I might argue that some divine commands are arbitrary and some are not. Richard Swinburne adopted this approach.³⁶ For example, suppose God commands that humans should rest one day out of seven (the fourth of the ten commandments). This command is arbitrary (why not rest one day out of ten?), but imposes a duty on humans because God is our supreme benefactor, and the reasonable commands of a benefactor should be obeyed. Suppose further that God prohibits murder because the proposition "murder is evil" is a necessary truth.³⁷ Since necessary truths are independent of God's will, and since it is wicked to command what is evil, God enforces these moral truths, but can't change them.³⁸ This does not imply a limitation of God's power because a coherent view of God's maximal power requires that it be understood within the context of logical possibility. It is no limitation of God's power to say that God cannot do what is logically impossible. In short, the defender of divine command ethics has a number of options available to avoid the force of the Euthyphro dilemma.

35. Adams, "A Modified Divine Command Theory of Ethical Wrongness."

36. Swinburne, *The Coherence of Theism*, 203–209.

37. See Necessary and Contingent, 24.

38. Swinburne has adopted the view taken by Aquinas. See, Aquinas, *Summa Contra Gentiles*, Book 1: God, ch. 95 and Book 2: Creation, ch. 25. See also Swinburne's brief discussion in *Is There a God?*, 15.

RIGHTS

The term *right* is ambiguous, and when its ambiguities are unrecognized, the result is darkness rather than light.[39] Consider the following propositions:

1. Adam has a right to be paid $50 by Beth.
2. Beth has a right to walk on the sidewalk.
3. Adam has a right to take money from Beth's bank account.
4. Beth has a right not to be disinherited by Adam.

In each case, the meaning of *right* is distinct. An American legal scholar, Wesley Newcomb Hohfeld, analyzed these differences in an enlightening way.[40] Ambiguity is eliminated by substituting in each instance another word that preserves the intended meaning.

1. Adam is *entitled* to be paid $50 by Beth.
2. Beth has *liberty* to walk on the sidewalk.
3. Adam has *power* to take money from Beth's bank account.
4. Beth is *immune* from being disinherited by Adam.

These distinctions should alert us always to inquire which meaning is intended when someone claims to pos-

---

39. "Right" is ambiguous in non-moral as well as in moral contexts—*right* as opposed to *left* and *right* (correct) as opposed to *incorrect*.

40. The best discussion of these distinctions is in Finnis, *Natural Law and Natural Rights*, 199–205. Finnis relies on and uses the distinctions originally made by Hohfeld, *Fundamental Legal Conceptions*.

sess a *right*.⁴¹ Notice further that, as Hohfeld demonstrated, each meaning entails a correlative term.

1. Adam is *entitled* to be paid $50 by Beth, if and only if, Beth has a *duty* to pay Adam $50. This would be the case if Beth borrowed $50 from Adam and promised to repay it.⁴² Notice that a *right* in this sense can never be to do or omit something yourself; it always entails someone else doing or omitting something.

2. Beth has *liberty* to walk on the sidewalk, if and only if, Adam is *not entitled* to have Beth stay off the sidewalk.⁴³ This would be the case if the sidewalk was a public space not owned by Adam.⁴⁴

3. Adam has *power* to take money from Beth's bank account, if and only if, Beth has a *liability* to have Adam take money from her account. This would be the case if a court of law granted Adam a monetary judgment against Beth for a debt she owed him and had failed to pay.

4. Beth is *immune* from being disinherited by Adam, if and only if, Adam has a *disability* to disinherit her. This would be the case if Adam and Beth were married.⁴⁵

---

41. There may be more than four meanings, but these four provide a useful starting place and demonstrate the distinct meanings.

42. Hohfeld called this a *claim-right*.

43. Hohfeld called this a *privilege*.

44. *Right* in this sense can also be expressed in a negative way: Adam (a philosophy professor) has *liberty* not to give Beth an A in her philosophy course, if and only if, Beth is *not entitled* to an A from Adam.

45. Although parents can disinherit their children, the law

Rights as *powers* and *immunities* normally require a constitution and code of laws, i.e., laws must be duly enacted to grant *powers* and *immunities*. However, if *human rights* exist, they are *entitlements* or *liberties* not granted by law, but possessed simply by virtue of being human. Do we possess such *entitlements* and *liberties*? Today, the international community in the west appears to assume that we do. The founders of the United States famously declared that God had endowed all humans with *unalienable rights* (rights that could not be sold or bargained away), and that among these were the right to life, liberty, and the pursuit of happiness. A Hohfeldian analysis leads us to interpret these in the following way. The right to life is an *entitlement*—everyone else in the world has a *duty* not to take away my life. The right to liberty is, of course, the declaration that others are not entitled to interfere with me. The right to pursue happiness is most naturally understood as a liberty, not an entitlement. No one has a duty to provide me with happiness, but others are not entitled to interfere with my pursuit of it.

When analyzed in this way, both legal rights and human rights make sense, but just as importantly one is able to see the fatuousness of many declarations of rights. For example, the United Nations Universal Declaration of Human Rights asserts, "everyone has a right to meaningful work." What does this mean? Of course it doesn't mean that everyone has an *immunity* to meaningful work. Does it mean that everyone has the *power* or *liberty* to obtain meaningful work? That seems unlikely, because it's patently false. Does it mean everyone is *entitled* to meaningful work? If so,

---

prohibits spouses from disinheriting each other.

someone has a duty to provide each of us with meaningful work. Who would that be? Do my fellow citizens have such a duty? It is hard to see how. Not even my parents or spouse have such a duty.

Similarly, various political or religious figures have occasionally declared that everyone has a right to healthcare. It's incoherent to say that everyone has an *immunity* to healthcare. If everyone has the *power* to obtain healthcare, we need not concern ourselves with it. It may be that everyone has *liberty* to acquire healthcare, but if so that hardly seems worth saying. The only thing that can be meant is that each of us is *entitled* to it. But that means someone has a duty to provide me with it. Once again, who would that be? Providing me with healthcare might be a very good thing for my fellow citizens to do, but it is difficult to see how they have a duty to do so.

6

Analytic Philosophy and Continental Philosophy[1]

IN THE western world today, philosophy in general and philosophers in particular are often described as either "analytic" or "continental." Analytic philosophy emerged in the early twentieth century when Bertrand Russell (1872–1970) and G. E. Moore (1873–1958), fellow students and then both professors at Cambridge University, worked their way out of the Hegelian idealism[2] they had been taught as students. Moore, whom Russell influenced to pursue philosophy, began this work by analyzing rigorously the metaphysical propositions of idealism.[3] Once he considered these propositions in light of *common sense* and the *ordinary meaning of words*, he concluded that they were certainly false. *Common sense* and the *ordinary meaning of words* thus became the first two ingredients in analytic philosophy.[4] Russell suggested that "the achievements of

1. The distinction between analytic and continental philosophy is widely accepted among western philosophers, but it has been interestingly challenged. See the fascinating discussion 'continental' and 'analytic' in *The Oxford Companion to Philosophy*.
2. See Realism and Idealism, 118 and Hegel, 41.
3. See Chapter 4, Metaphysics.
4. The concept of "common sense" as used in philosophy has roots

mathematicians who set to work to purge their subject of fallacies and slipshod reasoning" was a third ingredient.[5] These three elements, then—a high value placed on common sense, careful attention to the meaning of terms, and the use of new developments in logic—eliminated from Anglo-American philosophy much of what A. J. Ayer (1910–1989) characterized as "woolly uplift."[6]

Analytic philosophy was for a time influenced, and perhaps even dominated by, logical positivism, a form of empiricism[7] and skepticism similar to that of David Hume. Logical positivism grew out of the work of a group of philosophers who lived and taught in pre-World War II Vienna, Austria and who came to be known as the Vienna Circle. This group influenced, and was influenced by, Ludwig Wittgenstein (1889–1951), a fellow Viennese who subsequently studied under Russell at Cambridge. Logical positivism was popularized in Great Britain by A. J. Ayer, but it died a well deserved death when its center piece, the *verifiability criterion of meaning*, which asserted that only empirically verifiable statements are meaningful, was seen to fail its own test of meaningfulness and was mercifully abandoned.

---

in the Scottish Enlightenment and particularly in the philosophy of Thomas Reid. (See Realism and Idealism, 41.) Reid himself adopted Berkeley's idealism early in his life, but then rejected it after asking himself what evidence there was for the doctrine. See Reid, *Essays on the Intellectual Powers of Man*, 142.

5. Russell, *History of Western Philosophy*, 780.

6. An interesting definition of analytic philosophers is those who "would have done philosophy the way Moore, Russell, and Wittgenstein did it if they had been doing philosophy when Moore, Russell, and Wittgenstein were." Introduction, in A. P. Martinich and David Sosa, eds., *A Companion to Analytic Philosophy*, 5.

7. See Rationalism and Empiricism, 33.

Among the developments in the final years of the twentieth century, which Russell never could have predicted and probably would not have welcomed, was the amazing revival of philosophy of religion using techniques honed by the pioneers of analytic philosophy. The result was that the final twenty-five years of the twentieth century proved to be one of the most astonishingly creative periods for philosophy of religion in the history of western philosophy. This period of creativity continues unabated today.

The term "continent" in continental philosophy refers to the continent of Europe, primarily Germany and France. However, one of its most influential practitioners was Jacques Derrida (1930–2004), an Algerian born into a Jewish family who spent a considerable portion of his career teaching in the United States. Continental philosophy is not merely the kind of philosophy taught and practiced in Europe; it is more accurately understood as a style of philosophy influenced principally by thinkers with ties to Europe during the twentieth century.

The most important of the continental philosophers in the early part of the twentieth century was Martin Heidegger (1889–1976), whose monumental work *Sein und Zeit* (*Being and Time*) stands legitimately as one of the most influential books of the century. Arguably, three of the main themes of continental philosophy stem from him: *existentialism*, *phenomenology*, which he adopted and adapted from his teacher Edmund Husserl (1839–1938), and *deconstruction*, a philosophical activity that resists classification, but which became a central concern of continental philosophy.[8] The range of his influence can also be seen

8. Although the term "deconstruction" was formally introduced into philosophy by Derrida, it originated in Heidegger's philosophy

by his considerable effect on some Catholic and Protestant theologians. Just as analytic philosophy was, for a time, influenced and dominated by logical positivism, so continental philosophy was, for a time, influenced, and perhaps dominated, by existentialism. Jean Paul Sartre, the French philosopher, novelist, and playwright, is the most famous existentialist philosopher.

In the last decades of the twentieth century, Jacques Derrida became the most quoted continental philosopher. Although some consider his main influence to have been on literary criticism, he was a noted proponent of deconstruction. The animosity between the analytic and continental traditions, or at least their strikingly disparate approaches to philosophy, was exemplified in 1992 when a controversy broke out at Cambridge University caused by the award to Derrida of an honorary doctorate.

One way to get a sense of the difference between analytic and continental philosophy is by reading a representative of each. What follow are fairly typical examples. Roderick Chisholm, an analytic philosopher, wrote the first and Martin Heidegger, a continental philosopher, wrote the second.

> We can formulate some of the philosophical issues that are involved here by distinguishing two pairs of questions. These are:
> A. "What do we know? What is the *extent* of our knowledge?"

---

who attempted what he termed the *Destruktion* of the history of ontology. This should not be confused with "destruction" as understood in English. For an interesting discussion see "deconstruction" in Honderich, *The Oxford Guide to Philosophy*.

B. "How are we to decide *whether* we know? What are the *criteria* of knowledge?

If you happen to know the answers to the first of these pairs of questions, you may have some hope of being able to answer the second. Thus, if you happen to know which are the good apples and which are the bad ones, then maybe you could explain to some other person how he could go about deciding whether or not he has a good apple or a bad one. But if you don't know the answer to the first of these pairs of questions—if you don't know what things you know or how far your knowledge extends—it is difficult to see how you could possibly figure out an answer to the second.[9]

Dasein, as constituted by disclosedness, is essentially in the truth. Disclosedness is a kind of Being which is essential to Dasein. *'There is' truth only in so far as Dasein is and so long as Dasein is*. Entities are uncovered only *when* Dasein *is*; and only so long as Dasein *is*, are they disclosed. Newton's laws, the principle of contradiction, any truth whatever—these are true only as long as Dasein *is*. Before there was any Dasein, there was no truth; nor will there be any after Dasein is no more. For in such a case truth as disclosedness, uncovering, and uncoveredness, *cannot be*.[10]

---

9. Chisholm, "The Problem of the Criterion," 29.
10. Heidegger, *Being and Time*, 269.

7

Great Philosophers You Should Know

ANYONE'S LIST of the most influential philosophers in western intellectual history will include the following twelve philosophers, and every educated person should know something about them. Individual professors of philosophy may think I should have included others, but no one will believe I should have left someone out. With the exception of Augustine, who wrote one of the greatest autobiographies of all time, we know more about the lives of modern philosophers, beginning with Descartes, than we know about the ancient or medieval philosophers. But interesting details are known about the lives of all twelve philosophers included here.

Each entry begins first with a life chronology, the information for which I gathered from a variety of sources including biographies, biographical sketches, and works of general history. Second, I have explained why each philosopher is famous. Third, I have listed the philosophers' major works. There is general agreement regarding which books count as the major works, although, in every case, the philosopher wrote considerably more that would reward close study. Finally, I have suggested what I think a beginning student ought to buy to build his or her library and make rapid progress in understanding each philosopher. Except in the case of Hegel (in my view), the place to begin is always with the writing of the philosopher himself.[1] When you subsequently begin to read secondary sources, read first expositors that are sympathetic to the philosopher; they are most likely to be fair. If you begin by reading a secondary source that is highly critical, you are bound to get an unbalanced view. This doesn't mean you should avoid critical expositions; it means only that it would be unwise to start there. To give only one example, Jonathan Bennett's *Kant's Analytic* and *Kant's Dialectic* are outstanding critical expositions of Kant's *Critique of Pure Reason,* but no beginning student should start with them. Begin rather with Stephan Korner's *Kant*, an exposition that is understandable, sympathetic, and fair.

In compiling these outlines, I have aimed at three goals: to include as much information as possible in a brief compass, to recite the major facts known about the lives of each philosopher, and to leave out all salacious details, which might be interesting, but are irrelevant to philosophy.[2]

---

1. This is not possible with Socrates because he wrote nothing, or at least nothing we still have.

2. There are salacious details known about the lives of many, though not all modern philosophers. If you are interested in the tabloid newspaper version of their lives, consult general works of history and comprehensive biographies.

SOCRATES (C. 469-399 BC)

He "was perhaps the most original, influential, and controversial figure in the history of Greek thought."[3]

LIFE CHRONOLOGY:

c. 469 Born in Athens.

432 Member of the Athenian army when it besieged Potidaea.[4] ". . . and while there (he) is said to have remained a whole night without changing his position, and to have won the prize of valour."[5]

431 Peloponnesian War began (Athens v. Sparta).

424 Fought as a hoplite with the Athenian army in the battle of Delium (Athens lost).[6] ". . . and when in the battle of Delium Xenophon had fallen from his horse, he stepped in and saved his life."[7]

407 Plato became his student.

406 Battle of Arginusae. Following the Athenian naval triumph, captains of victorious triremes (Greek battle ships) failed to pick up the dead and rescue men from twelve wrecked triremes. Generals in charge of the battle were put on trial for their lives. Socrates alone

---

3. Edwards, ed., *The Encyclopedia of Philosophy*, s.v. "Socrates."

4. Plato, *Symposium*, 219e6, in Cooper, ed., *Plato: Complete Works*.

5. Laertius, *Lives of the Eminent Philosophers*, Vol. 1, 153.

6. Plato, *Symposium*, 220e ff and *Laches*, 181b, in Cooper, ed., *Plato: Complete Works*. Kagan discusses this battle in *The Peloponnesian War*, 167–170.

7. Laertius, *Lives of the Eminent Philosophers*, Vol. 1, 153.

(who was serving as a council member for that year, and, by coincidence, was the presiding officer that day) objected to an illegal motion to sentence the generals to death by a single vote.[8]

404 Peloponnesian War ended (Athens surrendered to Sparta).

399 Indicted, tried, convicted, sentenced to death by an Athenian jury and executed in Athens after his refusal to attempt an escape.

FAMOUS BECAUSE:

1. He was Plato's teacher and a character in the majority of Plato's dialogues.
2. Aristophanes caricatured him in his play *Clouds* (first produced in 423 BC).
3. Athenians indicted him on two charges. According to Diogenes Laertius, the indictment read as follows: "This indictment and affidavit is sworn by Meletus, the son of Meletus of Pitthos, against Socrates, the son of Sophroniscus of Alopece: Socrates is guilty of refusing to recognize the gods recognized by the state (*polis*), and of introducing other new divinities. He is also guilty of corrupting the youth. The penalty demanded is death."[9]

---

8. Plato, *Apology*, 32b-c, in Cooper, ed., *Plato: Complete Works*. Kagan discusses this incident in *The Peloponnesian War*, 461–66.

9. Laertius, *Lives of the Eminent Philosophers*, Vol. 1, 171. In Plato's dialogue *Euthyphro*, Socrates talks about the accusations against him. He is somewhat oblique regarding the charge of corrupting the youth (2c–2d), but regarding the other charge, he says that Meletus "charges me with making new gods, and not believing in the old ones." 3b.

4. The Athenian jury found him guilty and condemned him to death. Following his conviction, he proposed that his penalty be "free meals in the Prytaneum."[10] At Plato's urging, he amended this to a fine of thirty minas.[11] In the end, Socrates drank the hemlock as required and died.

5. His moral character is vividly seen in his acceptance of the death sentence and his refusal to escape from Athens and live in exile, although his friends urged him to do so.[12]

Major Works:

There are no extant works by Socrates.

What to Buy:

Reeve, C. D. C., Editor. *The Trials of Socrates: Six Classic Texts.* Indianapolis: Hackett Publishing Company, 2002. This is an excellent and reasonably priced introduction to Socrates. It contains the complete texts of the Platonic dialogues *Euthyphro* and *Crito*, as well as the *Apology* of Socrates and the death scene from *Phaedo*. It also contains Aristophanes' play *Clouds* and Xenophon's *Socrates Defense to the Jury*.

Vlastos, G. *Socrates: Ironist and Moral Philosopher.* Ithaca: Cornell University Press, 1991. This may well be the best book on Socrates written in the twentieth century.

---

10. Plato, *Apology*, 37a, in Cooper, ed., *Plato: Complete Works*.
11. Ibid., 38b8.
12. The account of this is given in Plato's dialogue *Crito*.

PLATO (C. 427–347 BC)

"The safest general characterization of the European philosophical tradition is that it consists of a series of footnotes to Plato."[13]

Life Chronology:

- c. 427 Born in Athens to a noble family; his father was a friend of Pericles (c. 495–429 BC), a Greek general and statesman).
- 407 Became a pupil of Socrates when he was twenty years old, but probably knew him from boyhood.
- 406 May have fought at Arginusae during the Peloponnesian War.[14]
- 404 Athens surrendered and the Peloponnesian War ended; Tyranny of the Thirty was established—Plato's relatives were leaders.
- 399 Present at Socrates' trial, but absent at Socrates execution because of illness. He left Athens in disgust after Socrates' execution and abandoned any lingering political aspirations in Athens.
- 388/7 Made his first visit to Italy and then Sicily, where he became friends with Dion, brother-in-law of Dionysius I, the Tyrant of Syracuse.
- 388/7 Some claim that because Plato angered Dionysius I, he was sold into slavery and then ransomed by Annicerius of Cyrene.[15]

---

13. Whitehead, *Process and Reality*, 39.

14. For an account of this battle, see Kagan, *The Peloponnesian War*, 454–61.

15. Laertius, *Lives of the Eminent Philosophers*, Vol. 1, 293–95.

388/7 Upon return to Athens, he founded a school known as the Academy. Some call this the first European university because the subjects of study included mathematics, astronomy, and the physical sciences, as well as philosophy.[16]

367 Aristotle entered the Academy. Plato made a second visit to Syracuse apparently at the invitation of Dion, uncle of the new king, to educate young Dionysius II.

361 Made a final visit to Syracuse at the invitation of Dionysius II.

347 Died at Athens while in the process of publishing the *Laws*.

Famous because:

1. He wrote masterful dialogues that are the foundational documents of western philosophy.[17] Scholars have divided these into three periods (early, middle, and late). Of forty-three works which claim Plato's authorship, twenty-six are considered genuine, three are uncertain, and fourteen are considered not genu-

---

16. That it was not the *first university* is disputed by some who say it was not a university, and by others who say it was not the first. Isocrates' school began eight years earlier, and the Pythagorean school of Crotona dates back to 520 BC. See, Durant, *The Life of Greece*, 511.

17. "The Platonic dialogues are a representation of the world; they are a cosmos in themselves . . . The dialogues are constructed with an almost unbelievable care and subtlety. The drama is everywhere, even in what seem to be the most stock responses or the most purely theoretical disquisitions." These are Allan Bloom's words from his Preface to *The Republic of Plato*, xxii.

ine. In addition, there are letters and epigrams, some of which are considered genuine and others not.

2. The *Republic*, arguably his greatest dialogue, is a quest for the meaning of justice. In the process of seeking what it means for a person to be just, Plato draws a lengthy analogy between a properly ordered human soul and a properly ordered city.

3. The most famous allegory in all of philosophy is Plato's allegory of the cave which is found in Book VII of the *Republic*. The story represents the soul's assent toward "the idea of the good."[18]

4. He is one of two major sources for Socrates' thought.[19]

5. He was Aristotle's teacher.

MAJOR WORKS:

Apology, Crito, Phaedo (Probably historical accounts of Socrates)

Republic

Symposium

Laws

WHAT TO BUY:

Plato, *Complete Works*. Edited with Introduction and Notes by John M. Cooper Indianapolis: Hackett Publishing Company, 1997. This collection gathers together modern translations of all genuine and dis-

---

18. Plato, *The Republic of Plato*, 514a ff.

19. The other major source is Xenephon. See Xenephon, *Conversations of Socrates*.

puted works by Plato. It is by far the best edition of the complete works in English.

Plato, *The Republic of Plato*. Translated with notes and interpretive essay by Allan Bloom. New York: Basic Books, 1991. This is a very readable translation of Plato's most famous work. The interpretive essay makes this edition worth owning on its own.

Kraut, Richard. *The Cambridge Companion to Plato*. New York: Cambridge University Press, 1992.

ARISTOTLE (384–322 BC)

He "fixed the main outlines of the classification of the sciences in the form which they still retain, and carried most of the sciences to a further point than they had hitherto reached; in some of them, such as logic he may fairly claim to have had no predecessor . . ."[20]

LIFE CHRONOLOGY:

- 384 Born in Stagira on the Chalcidice peninsula. His father was court physician to Amyntas II, Philip of Macedon's father and the grandfather of Alexander the Great.
- 368/7 Sent to Athens (age seventeen or eighteen) where he began to study at Plato's Academy. Remained in close association with the Academy for twenty years until Plato's death in 348/7.
- 348 Plato's nephew, Seusippus, was chosen to succeed Plato as head of the Academy. Aristotle left Athens and accepted the invitation of Hermeias, former fellow-student at the Academy, to come to Mysia (Asia Minor). He subsequently married Pythias, the niece of Hermeias.
- 345 Moved to the island of Lesbos where, at least some of the time, he studied biological specimens.
- 343/2 Invited by Philip of Macedon to become tutor of his son Alexander (then thirteen years old). Aristotle probably tutored Alexander only until 340 when Alexander was appointed regent for his father.

20. Ross, *Aristotle*, 5.

340 Probably settled in Stagira and resumed his biological research. According to Plutarch, when Philip of Macedon sent for Aristotle to tutor Alexander, Philip "repeopled his native city Stagira, which he had caused to be demolished a little before, and restored all the citizens, who were in exile or slavery, to their habitations."[21]

335/4 Returned to Athens and organized the Lyceum—a new school. He lived in Athens as an alien without political rights and was suspect because of his connections to Macedonia.

323 Fled from Athens after Alexander's death in Babylon.

322 Died in Chalcis in Euboea. He asked to be buried next to his first wife Pythias, who had died in childbirth.

FAMOUS BECAUSE:

1. He was Plato's greatest student. According to Plutarch, when Philip of Macedon requested that Aristotle tutor Alexander, he was "the most learned and most celebrated philosopher of his time . . ."[22]

2. His comprehensive philosophy based on empiricism was a response to, and criticism of, Plato's rationalism.[23]

3. He wrote major treatises on every area of philosophy including logic, metaphysics, and ethics, as well as major treatises on political philosophy and rhetoric.

21. Plutarch, *The Lives of the Noble Grecians and Romans*, 543.
22. Ibid.
23. See Rationalism and Empiricism 33.

4. His *Nicomachean Ethics* has been called the greatest book on moral philosophy ever written.
5. "To [Aristotle] science and philosophy owe a multitude of terms that in their Latin forms have facilitated learned communication and thought—*principle, maxim, faculty, mean, category, energy, motive, habit, end* . . ."[24]

MAJOR WORKS:

De Interpretatione
Prior and Posterior Analytics
Physics
Metaphysics
Nicomachean Ethics
Politics
Rhetoric

WHAT TO BUY:

Aristotle: Selections. Translated with Introduction, Notes, and Glossary by T. Irwin and G. Fine. Indianapolis: Hackett Publishing Company, 1995. This is a modern translation of significant portions of Aristotle's major works. The glossary makes this edition particularly valuable.

Barnes, J. ed. *The Cambridge Companion to Aristotle*. New York: Cambridge University Press, 1995.

---

24. Durant, *The Life of Greece*, 537 (Emphasis in the original).

Ross, David. *Aristotle*. With new introduction by J. L. Ackrill. New York: Routledge, 1995. If you want to understand Aristotle, buy this book.

AUGUSTINE (AD 354–430)

"In Western Christendom no other author had more sustained authority in philosophy and theology than did Augustine."[25]

LIFE CHRONOLOGY:

354 Born in Thagaste (now Souk-Ahras, Algeria).

373 Read Cicero's *Hortensius* (a lost work) which changed his life, and began his search for wisdom. Shortly afterwards, he adopted Manichaeism.[26]

384 Appointed professor of Rhetoric in Milan, Italy.

386 Became a Christian through the influence of Ambrose (Bishop of Milan).

388 Returned to Thagaste.

391 Arrived in Hippo (now Annaba, Algeria) to found a monastery and was ordained a priest.

395 Became Bishop of Hippo.

401 Completed writing his *Confessions*.

410 Gothic Army, led by Alaric, entered Rome.

426 Completed writing the *City of God* (which he had begun in 413).

430 Died at Hippo as Vandals were invading the city.

---

25. Weinberg, *A Short History of Medieval Philosophy*, 45.

26. Mani (AD 216–77) was a Persian dualist who taught that there were two coeternal powers Light (good) and Darkness (evil). Augustine was an adherent for nine years because he thought only the Manichaeans could answer the question "From what cause do we do evil?"

Famous because:

1. His book, *Confessions*, stands as one of the greatest autobiographies of all time and explains his early life and conversion to Christianity.
2. He made major contributions to many philosophical problems including time, human freewill as it relates to God's foreknowledge, and the nature of evil.
3. His book, *City of God*, which required over twenty years to write, contrasts the degradation of pagan Rome with the glory of the City of God.
4. He was a Christian Platonist for whom Plato was a path away from Manichaeism and toward Christianity.
5. He refuted skepticism by arguing that three kinds of propositions were invulnerable to attack: the existence of oneself, mathematical truths, and moral truths.[27]

Major Works:

Confessions

Concerning the City of God Against the Pagans

---

27. Weinberg, *A Short History of Medieval Philosophy*, 33–34. Weinberg points out that Augustine's refutation of skepticism precedes Descartes' famous *cogito ergo sum* (I think, therefore I am) by many centuries. Augustine argued that in order to be deceived one must exist, and about that one cannot be in doubt. Weinberg also claims that this argument can be traced back to Plato's *Theatetus*.

What to Buy:

Everyone should own and read Augustine's two major works, the *Confessions* and *City of God*. Many translations and editions of both are available.

> Brown, Peter. *Augustine of Hippo*. Berkeley: University of California Press, 1975. This is still the most thorough and insightful biography of Augustine.
>
> Stump, E, and N. Kretzmann, eds. *The Cambridge Companion to Augustine*. New York: Cambridge University Press, 2001.

ANSELM (1033-1109)

"Anselm possessed a subtlety and originality that rank him among the most penetrating medieval thinkers (along with Augustine, Aquinas, Duns Scotus, and William of Ockham) and explain the perennial fascination with his ideas."[28]

LIFE CHRONOLOGY:

1033 Born in Aosta in northern Italy.

1054 Year of the Great Schism—churches in the east, under patriarch Michael Cerularius, and churches in the west, under Pope Leo IX, split from each other.

1059 Entered the monastery at Bec in central Normandy as a student.

1060 Became a monk at Bec.

1066 Norman invasion of England on September 28, and Battle of Hastings on October 14, wherein King Harold II of England was defeated by William the Conqueror.

1077/8 Completed Proslogion.

1078 Became Abbot of Bec.

Early 1090s Began controversy with Roscelin[29] (1050-1125), which led to first version of the *De Incarnatione Verbi* (*On the Incarnation of the Word*).

---

28. Honderich, ed., *The Oxford Guide to Philosophy*, s.v. "Anselm of Canterbury, St."

29. Or Roscellinus, who is regarded as the founder of medieval nominalism (See Universal and Particular, 38-39). Roscelin was accused of teaching Tritheism (believing in three gods) rather than the Trinity.

1093 Nominated Archbishop of Canterbury by King William II. Problems arose over respective roles of church and state.

1097–1100 Went to Rome to ask for the Pope's advice on resolving his dispute with the King.

1098 Completed *Cur Deus Homo* (*Why God Became Man*). He spoke to Council of Bari at the Pope's request to try to mend the schism between the eastern and western churches. He argued for the western view that the Holy Spirit proceeds from Father and Son.

1102 Published *De processione Spiritus Sancti* (*The Procession of the Holy Spirit*) and *Letters on the Sacraments*.

1103-7 Had a dispute with King Henry I and was sent into exile.

1106 Returned to England.

1109 Died at Canterbury.

FAMOUS BECAUSE:

1. The "ontological argument" for God's existence was his invention—an argument that moves from the concept of God's *being* to God's *existence*. In every generation, this argument seems to produce powerful critics and staunch defenders.[30]

---

30. About the ontological argument, Charles Hartshorne has written this: "It was stated in a few pages, and elaborated—in response to criticism—in a few more. Yet even these few pages have been far too many for the Arguments' detractors to read." Introduction to Anslem of Canterbury, *St. Anselm: Basic Writings*, 3.

2. He articulated the ideal of "faith seeking understanding" when he wrote, "For I do not seek to understand, so that I may believe; but I believe so that I may understand. For I believe this also that 'unless I believe I shall not understand.'"[31]
3. He articulated a "satisfaction" theory of the atonement, wherein humans owe satisfaction to God, but cannot make it; God (as all-powerful) can make satisfaction, but doesn't owe it. Hence, the necessity of a God/Man to make satisfaction (*Cur Deus Homo*).

Major Works:

Monologion

Proslogion

De Incarnatione Verbi (*On the Incarnation of the Word*).

Cur Deus Homo (*Why God Became Man*).

What to Buy:

Anselm of Canterbury. *Anselm of Canterbury: The Major Works*. Edited with Introduction by Brian Davies and G. R. Evans. Oxford: Oxford University Press, 2008. This is a compact and affordable edition of modern translations of Anselm's major works.

---

31. Anselm of Canterbury. "Proslogium 1" in *The Major Works*, 87. The final quotation is designated by Anselm as coming from Isaiah 7:9, which in a modern English translation reads, "If you do not firm in faith, you will not stand at all." (NIV)

AQUINAS (1225–1274)

"Somewhere, right now, there are people poring over his texts— over seven hundred years after his death."[32]

Life Chronology:

- c.1225 Born in Roccasecca in Kingdom of Naples (Italy), the youngest of seven sons.
- 1231 Sent to Monte Cassino at about five years of age to begin his studies with the Benedictine monks. He stayed there for about nine years.
- 1239-44 Studied the liberal arts at the University of Naples.
- 1244 Joined the Order of Preachers (Dominicans) against his family's wishes. At his mother's request (his father had recently died), two of his brothers who were army officers took him prisoner. Only after the Dominicans appealed to the Pope and the Emperor was he released.
- 1245-48 Studied at the University of Paris with Albert the Great (c.1200–1280).
- 1248-52 Albert the Great was sent to Cologne and he took Thomas with him. Four year later, he received his baccalaureate.
- 1252 Sent to the University of Paris for advanced study in theology. He also lectured on the Christian scriptures and on the *Sentences* of Peter Lombard.

---

32. McInerny, *A First Glance at St. Thomas Aquinas*, 1.

1256 Awarded magistrate (doctorate) in theology at Paris. This required a special papal dispensation because he was only thirty-one years old and a magistrate in theology was normally not awarded until the age of thirty-four.

1257-59 Taught as a member of faculty of theology at the University of Paris. During this time he began work on the *Summa Contra Gentiles*.

1259-68 Taught at various Dominican monasteries in the vicinity of Rome. While there he wrote the first part of the *Summa Theologiae*.

1265-69 Wrote commentaries on many of Aristotle's works.

1267 Began work on *Summa Theologiae*.

1268-72 Returned to University of Paris for second professorate in theology. While there, he wrote the second part of *Summa Theologiae* and more commentaries on Aristotle's works.

1272 Regent Master at University of Naples.

1273 On December 6, he had a mystical experience during Mass and ceased writing and teaching. He reportedly said, "All I have written seems to me like so much straw compared with what I have seen and with what has been revealed to me."[33]

1274 Pope Gregory X sent him to the Council of Lyons in France. He became ill on the way and died at the Cistercian monastery of Fossanova on March 7.

---

33. Copleston, *Aquinas*, 10.

Famous because:

1. By using the newly rediscovered Aristotelian works as the philosophical foundation for expounding Christian doctrine, he "Christianized" Aristotle.
2. The Five Ways (*Quinque Viae*) are his most famous arguments whereby he asserted in the *Summa Theologiae* 1A, 2, 3 that one can demonstrate God's existence. The first four are versions of the cosmological argument in which God's existence is inferred from change, causation, contingency, and gradations observed in things. The fifth way is a version of the teleological argument in which God's existence is inferred from order observed in nature.
3. He wrote two massive summations of theology that remain in print and provide the intellectual basis for Roman Catholic philosophy and theology.

Major Works:

On the Truth of the Catholic Faith Against the Gentiles (known as *Summa Contra Gentiles*)

Summa Theologiae

What to Buy:

Aquinas, Thomas. *Summa of the Summa*. Edited and Annotated by Peter Kreeft. San Francisco: Ignatius Press, 1990. Kreeft has abridged the *Summa Theologiae* and written footnotes that explain and illuminate the most difficult passages. This is the best introduction to the philosophy of Aquinas with which I am acquainted.

Kretzmann, N., and E. Stump., eds. *The Cambridge Companion to Aquinas*. New York: Cambridge University Press, 1993.

Chesterton, G. K. *St. Thomas Aquinas: "The Dumb Ox."* New York: Doubleday, 1956. This is a highly readable and entertaining biography.

DESCARTES (1596–1650)

"[H]is main ideas can be so concisely expressed that they could be written on the back of a postcard [man is a thinking mind; matter is extension in motion]; and yet they were so revolutionary that they changed the course of philosophy for centuries."[34]

LIFE CHRONOLOGY:

- 1596 Born in the town of La Haye, in Touraine, France. La Haye was later renamed La Haye-Descartes, and now is named simply Descartes.
- 1604 Educated at the Jesuit college of La Fleche.
- 1616 Graduated from the University of Poitiers with degrees in civil and canon law.
- 1618 The Thirty Years' War began (initially a dispute between Protestants and Catholics in Bohemia). After graduating from the University of Poitiers, he went to Holland and served in the army of Maurice of Nassau.
- 1619 Went to Germany and enlisted in the Duke of Bavaria's army. According to *Discourse on Method, Part Two*, it was during this time that he spent a day of leisure meditating in a stove-heated room. This led to Meditation One of *Meditations on First Philosophy*.
- 1628 In Paris, he publicly attacked the view that science could only be established on probabilities. He wrote *Rules for the Direction of the Mind* (not published until

---

34. Kenny, ed., *The Oxford Illustrated History of Western Philosophy*, 113.

1701), and then returned to Holland where he lived for over twenty years.

1629 Wrote *Discourse on Method*, but did not publish it for eight more years.

1634 Completed a scientific work, *Le Monde (The World)* but had it suppressed because it endorsed the Copernican theory of the solar system for which Galileo had just been condemned.

1637 Published his work on dioptics, geometry, and meteorology prefaced by his brief *Discourse on Method*.

1641 Published *Meditationes de Prima Philosophia* (*Meditations on First Philosophy*).

1644 Published *Principia Philosophiae* (*Principles of Philosophy*) an edited version of *The World*.

1649 Accepted the invitation of Queen Christina of Sweden to join her court and teach her philosophy. He published *Le Passions de l'ame* (*The Passions of the Soul*),which grew out of his correspondence with Princess Elizabeth of Palatine, niece of Charles I, who challenged his assertion that the soul can move the body.

1650 Died of pneumonia, perhaps because of the Swedish climate and Queen Christina's demand that she be instructed at five a.m. He was suspected of influencing the queen to convert to Catholicism.

FAMOUS BECAUSE:

1. He is considered to be the first modern philosopher and founder of modern rationalism.[35]
2. He founded (invented/discovered) analytic geometry. The x, y, z coordinates used to define position in three-dimensional space are still referred to as Cartesian coordinates.
3. His assertion "I think, therefore I am" (*cogito ergo sum*) is widely known, widely quoted, and almost as widely misunderstood.[36] It has been called the most famous sentence in philosophy.[37]
4. In his *Discourse on Method: Part One* he wrote "Good sense is, of all things among men, the most equally distributed; for everyone thinks himself so abundantly provided with it, that those even who are the most difficult to satisfy in everything else, do not usually desire a larger measure of this quality than they already possess."[38]

35. See Rationalism and Empiricism, 33.

36. The French version of this phrase appeared first in his *Discourse on Method (Part Four)*. " . . . while I thus wished to think that all was false, it was absolutely necessary that I, who thus thought, should be somewhat; and as I observed that this truth, *I think, hence I am*, was so certain and of such evidence, that no ground of doubt however extravagant, could be alleged by the skeptics capable of shaking it, I concluded that I might, without scruple, accept it as the first principle of the philosophy of which I was in search."

37. "It was intended not as a syllogism, but as an immediate and irrefragable experience, the clearest and most distinct idea that we can ever have." Durant, *The Age of Reason*, 639.

38. Of this sentence, it has been said that it is to philosophy what the first sentence of Jane Austen's *Pride and Prejudice* is to the novel.

Major Works:

Discourse on Method
Meditations on First Philosophy
The Principles of Philosophy

What to Buy:

Everyone should own and read *Discourse on Method* and *Mediations on First Philosophy*. The latter is widely anthologized, the former less so. Both are in print and available in various translations and editions.

Cottingham, J., ed. *The Cambridge Companion to Descartes*. Cambridge: Cambridge University Press, 1992.

The latter reads: "It is a truth universally acknowledged, that a single man in possession of a good fortune, must be in want of a wife."

LOCKE (1632–1704)

"Locke, in giving theoretical expression to the principles underlying the Glorious Revolution of 1688-9, inspiring the political thought of the French Enlightenment (although not that of the Jacobins of the French Revolution) and in providing the intellectual bone-structure of the American Declaration of Independence, must be acknowledged to be the most influential of political thinkers, above even Plato, Aristotle, Hobbes, Rousseau, and Marx."[39]

LIFE CHRONOLOGY:

- 1632 Born in a rural area near Bristol, England.
- 1644 Began studies at Westminster School.
- 1649 Charles I was executed in London.
- 1652 Won a scholarship to Christ Church College, Oxford.
- 1656 Received his bachelor's degree.
- 1658 Received his master's degree and remained at Oxford teaching successively: Greek, rhetoric, and moral philosophy.
- 1661 His father, an attorney, died and left him a small fortune.
- 1664 Began to study medicine.
- 1665 Was part of a diplomatic mission to Brandenburg.
- 1666 Began occasionally to practice medicine.
- 1667 Invited to become the personal physician of Anthony Ashley Cooper, who later became the first Earl of Shaftesbury.

39. Quinton, "Political Philosophy" in Kenny, ed., *The Oxford Illustrated History of Western Philosophy*, 323.

1668 Performed surgery on Lord Ashley and saved his life.

1670 Began writing his *Essay Concerning Human Understanding.*

1673–75 Was secretary to the Council of Trade and Plantations. During this time, he aided Shaftesbury, who was president of the Council, in drafting the "Fundamental Constitutions for Government of Carolina."

1675 When Shaftesbury fell from power, Locke went to France and studied there.

1679 When Shaftesbury was returned to power, Locke returned to London.

1680 Moved back to Oxford.

1683 After Shaftesbury was arrested and escaped to Holland, Locke also left Oxford for Holland.

1685 James II requested his extradition, claiming he had plotted to overthrow the king. He hid under the name of Dr. Van der Linden.

1686 James II offered him a pardon, but he refused to return to England.

1687 He apparently did join in a plot to replace James II with William III. This eventuated in the Glorious Revolution of 1688–89.[40]

1689 Returned to England where his *Letter Concerning Toleration* was published in English.

---

40. On the "Glorious Revolution" in general, see the chapter entitled "King James II and the Glorious Revolution" in Maurice Ashley, *England in the Seventeenth Century. The Pelican History of England: 6.*

1690 Published *Two Treatises of Government* and shortly afterward published his *Essay Concerning Human Understanding*, on which he had been working for twenty years. He was also appointed Commissioner of Appeals.

1696 Appointed Commissioner of Trade and Plantations.

1704 Died at Oates Manor in Essex.

FAMOUS BECAUSE:

1. His *Essay Concerning Human Understanding* was the foundation for modern empiricism in response to Descartes' rationalism.[41] He wrote, "Let us then suppose the mind to be, as we say, white paper, void of all characters, without ideas; how comes it to be furnished? . . . To this I answer in one word, from EXPERIENCE; in that all our knowledge is founded, and from that it ultimately derives itself."[42]

2. His *Second Treatise of Government* was the foundation for democracy in America and England.

MAJOR WORKS:

Letter Concerning Toleration
Essay Concerning Human Understanding
Two Treatises of Government

---

41. See Rationalism and Empiricism, 33f.

42. *An Essay Concerning Human Understanding*, Book II, Chapter 1, Section 2.

WHAT TO BUY:

Locke, John. *An Essay Concerning Human Understanding.* Edited by P. H. Nidditch. Oxford: Oxford University Press, 1975.

Locke, John. *Two Treatises of Government.* Edited with an Introduction and Notes by Peter Laslett. Cambridge: Cambridge University Press, 1999.

KANT (1724–1804)

"Over two thousand books and articles on Kant were published before his death in 1804. In our own times, an average of more than two hundred books and articles are added every year."[43]

Life Chronology:

1724 Born in Konigsberg, Prussia.

1732–40 Attended a pietist school (*Collegium Fredericianum*) directed by his Lutheran Pastor.

1740 Entered the University of Konigsberg. Against university regulations, he did not choose a major (and register as a student in one of the higher faculties). Rather, he attended lectures in all the faculties including the sciences, theology, and medicine. His favorite teacher, Martin Knutzen introduced him to the rationalism of Gottfried W. Leibniz (1646–1716) and Christian Wolff (1679–1750).

1746–55 Acted as tutor to three private families.

1755 Received his doctorate from Konigsberg University. Hume's (1711–76) *Enquiry Concerning Human Understanding* was published in German translation.

1755–70 Lectured at Konigsberg as a *privatdozent*. During this time he applied twice for a professorship, but was rejected.

1770 Appointed professor of logic and metaphysics at Konigsberg University. His inaugural dissertation

---

43. Beck, "Bibliographical Essay" in Kant, *Kant: Selections*, 469.

as professor was *On the Form and Principles of the Sensible and Intelligible World.*

1781 Published his *Critique of Pure Reason.* He claimed that it took him only four or five months to write the entire book. He was greatly disappointed by its initial reception, although today, by common consent, it is considered one of the most important books in the history of philosophy.

1783 Published *Prolegomena to Any Future Metaphysics.*

1785 Published *Grounding for the Metaphysics of Morals.*

1788 Published *Critique of Practical Reason.*

1789 His health began to decline.

1790 Published *Critique of Judgment.*

1793 Published *Religion Within the Bounds of Reason Alone.* He disputed with the Prussian government regarding liberty to express opinions regarding religion.

1975 Published *Perpetual Peace.*

1797 Retired from lecturing. Published *On an Alleged Right to Lie out of Altruism*, in which he famously (or infamously) argued that lying in order to save the life of an innocent person is morally wrong.

1804 After a gradual and difficult mental decline, he died in Konigsberg, and was buried in the Konigsberg Cathedral. In 1880, his body was interred in a chapel near the cathedral.

FAMOUS BECAUSE:

1. He attempted to find a middle way between the rationalism of Descartes, Leibniz, and Wolff, and the empiricism of Locke and Hume. He did this by means of an intellectual Copernican revolution, which consisted in a new approach to metaphysics and epistemology. The old assumption, shared by rationalists and empiricists, was that the external world dictated to the human mind what was real and what could be known. In its place, Kant asserted that humans would have more success if they replaced that assumption with the reverse. Assume, Kant said, that the human mind determines the form in which the world of appearances (the phenomenal world) can be experienced and what can be known about it.

2. In the *Critique of Pure Reason*, he offered powerful criticisms of the ontological, cosmological, and teleological arguments for God's existence.

3. He asserted that all rational beings (including God) have a duty to conform their lives to a moral principle he called the *categorical imperative*.[44] It can be articulated in various ways, among which is: "always treat other humans as ends and never as means."[45] Kant held that this principle, and this alone, was the foundation of all morality.

---

44. See Deontology, 66f.

45. Kant, *Grounding for the Metaphysics of Morals*, 430. Another articulation is: "I should never act except in such a way that I can also will that my maxim should become a universal law." 402.

4. He wrote, "I openly confess my recollection of David Hume was the very thing which many years ago first interrupted my dogmatic slumber and gave my investigations in the field of speculative philosophy a quite new direction."[46]

Major Works:

Critique of Pure Reason
Prolegomena to Any Future Metaphysics
Grounding for the Metaphysics of Morals
Critique of Practical Reason
Critique of Judgment
Religion Within the Bounds of Reason Alone

What to Buy:

No one can understand modern or post-modern philosophy without understanding Kant. The place to start is with two of his shorter works: *Prolegomena to Any Future Metaphysics* and *Grounding for the Metaphysics of Morals*. Various editions of these are available in English translation.

Korner, Stephan. *Kant*. New Haven, CT: Yale University Press, 1955. I cannot recommend this book too highly. Find a used copy; buy it and study it.

---

46. Kant, *Prolegomena*, 8. A challenge to any student of Kant—try to find any article or book written about Kant that does not contain this quote or part of this quote.

HEGEL (1770–1831)

"Hegel's own mature philosophy . . . is a dateless, inexplicable product of genius, not led up to quite understandably by the past of philosophy or by Hegel's own past."[47]

Life Chronology:

1770 Born in Stuttgart in Duchy of Wurttemberg.

1788 Left Stuttgart to study at Tubingen University's Theological Institute.

1789 French Revolution began, which Hegel initially embraced.

1793–1800 Held two tutorial positions, and began to develop his own ideas.

1796 Wrote a *Life of Jesus* (*Das Lebens Jesu*), which was unpublished until 1905.

1799 His father died leaving him a small legacy (3,154 florins), which relieved him of the need to tutor.

1801 Upon the recommendation of Schelling (1775–1854), he moved to Jena and was permitted to lecture at the University of Jena as a *privatdozent*.

1804 Appointed *professor extraordinarius* at Jena.

1805 Austrians and Russians defeated Napoleon at Austerlitz.

1806 Following the Battle of Jena (Napoleon vs. Prussia), he lost his teaching post as a consequence of economic circumstances.

1807 Published *Phenomenology of Spirit*.

47. Findlay, *Hegel: A Re-Examination*, 33.

Great Philosophers You Should Know   119

1808–16 Became Rector of a school in Nuremberg.

1816 Appointed to Chair of Philosophy at University of Heidelberg.

1817 Published *The Science of Logic* and *Encyclopedia of Philosophical Sciences.*

1818 Appointed to Chair of Philosophy at University of Berlin, where he remained until his death.

1831 Died during a cholera epidemic in Berlin.

Famous because:

1. He asserted that all things, including history, proceed according to the pattern of thesis, antithesis, and synthesis, which today is known as the *Hegelian dialectic.*[48]

2. His philosophy is a form of *idealism*[49], in that he opposed the distinction between thought and reality.

3. He was a major influence on (a) Kierkegaard (1813–1855) (an inveterate opponent), (b) Marx (1818–1883) and Marxism (the "left-wing" Hegelians), and (c) Heidegger, and through him contemporary continental philosophy.[50]

---

48. Dialectic was Plato's name for Socrates' method of seeking truth through disputation. Dialectic was Kant's name for the human tendency to draw contradictory conclusions. In distinction from both of these, dialectic was Hegel's name for the propensity of humans to transcend contradictions. See Roger Scruton's discussion of this in *From Descartes to Wittgenstein: A Short History of Modern Philosophy*, 167.

49. See Realism and Idealism, 41.

50. See Analytic and Continental Philosophy, 78.

Major Works:

Phenomenology of Spirit (sometimes called *Phenomenology of Mind*)
The Science of Logic
Encyclopedia of Philosophical Sciences
The Philosophy of Right

What to Buy:

Hegel's philosophy is notoriously difficult, so recommending a place to start or a book by him is risky. Probably you should not start with Hegel himself, but with a *sympathetic* and *fair* exposition of his philosophy. I recommend the discussion of Hegel in Robert Solomon's *From Rationalism to Existentialism*. (Lanham, MD: University Press of America, 1985), 39–67. This book is no longer in print but can be found in a good library, and can perhaps be purchased used.

Beiser, F. C. *The Cambridge Companion to Hegel and Nineteenth-Century Philosophy*. New York: Cambridge University Press, 2008.

HEIDEGGER (1889-1976)

"Heidegger's work is a mountain range which we are not yet in a position to climb. We are able, it is true, to go some distance along this or that path and in the process catch sight of much that is unusual and exciting—but all that is a far cry from a direct hike to the ridge."[51]

LIFE CHRONOLOGY:

1889 Born in Messkirch, Germany to Roman Catholic parents.

1903-6 Attended the *Gymnasium* at Constance.

1906-9 Attended the *Gymnasium* at Freiburg.

1907 Franz Brentano's *On the Manifold Meaning of Being According to Aristotle*, (published in 1862) was given to him by the pastor of Trinity Church in Constance. According to Heidegger, this was "the chief help and guide of my first awkward attempts to penetrate into philosophy."[52]

1909-11 Studied theology at University of Freiburg.

19011-13 Switched to the study of philosophy.

1916 Wrote his habilitation dissertation on Duns Scotus (*Die Kategorien und Bedeutungslehre des Duns Scotus*).

1916-17 Lectured as *privatdozent* at Freiburg.

1917 Married Elfriede Petri.

---

51. Biemel, *Martin Heidegger*, 177.
52. Heidegger, *Martin Heidegger: Basic Writings*, 3.

1917–18 Served in German army until the end of World War I.

1918–22 Was Edmund Husserl's assistant at University of Freiburg

1922 Appointed as an associate professor (*professor extraordinarius*) at University of Marburg, where New Testament critic Rudolf Bultmann was a colleague. They apparently attended one another's classes. Among his most famous students at Marburg were Hans-Georg Gadamer, Hannah Arendt, and Leo Strauss. He built his cottage at Todtnauberg where the greater part of *Being and Time* was apparently written.

1927 Published *Being and Time* (*Sein und Zeit*), his first and most important book.

1928 Elected to replace Husserl at the University of Freiburg where he remained for the rest of his academic life.

1933 On April 21 was appointed Rector of the University of Freiburg. On May 1, he joined the Nazi party. On May 27, as rector, he gave a now infamous *Rektoratsrede* or inaugural address entitled "The Self-Assertion of the German University" (*Die Selbstbehauptung der deutschen Universitat*). This address is used by Heidegger's critics as evidence of his initial warm reception of National Socialism.[53]

---

53. About this, the comment of Hannah Arendt, a former student, is worth quoting. "We who wish to honor the thinkers ... can hardly help finding it striking and perhaps exasperating that Plato and Heidegger, when they entered into human affairs, turned to tyrants and Fuhrers ... For the attraction to the tyrannical can be demonstrated theoretically in many of the great thinkers (Kant is the great exception)." "Heidegger

1934 Resigned as rector but remained on the faculty, and also remained a member of the Nazi party until the war's end.

1944 Required to perform *Volkssturm*, or compulsory national service.

1945 Left the Nazi party, but was banned by the French Occupation Authority from teaching in Germany. He continued to give public lectures.

1947 Published *Letter on Humanism* (*Platons Lehre von der Wahrheit. Mit eniem Brief uber den Humanismus*).

1951 The ban from teaching in Germany was lifted. He was granted professor emeritus status at Freiburg.

1953 Published *Introduction to Metaphysics* (*Einfuhrung in die Metaphysik*).[54]

1962 Made a trip to Greece.

1976 Died on May 26.

Famous because:

1. His first and most well known book, *Being and Time*, was a foundational work in continental philosophy.[55]

---

at Eighty," 303.

54. Heidegger's critics have pointed to the following quote as troublesome: "The works that are being peddled about nowadays as the philosophy of National Socialism but have nothing whatever to do with the inner truth and greatness of this movement (namely the encounter between global technology and modern man)—have all been written by men fishing in the troubled waters of 'values' and 'totalities.'" Heidegger, *Introduction to Metaphysics*, 166.

55. See Analytic Philosophy and Continental Philosophy, 78f

2. The *Seinsfrage*, or "question of being," was the focus of his philosophical work. He urged that the history of western philosophy had lost sight of the primal concept of "being" as compared with "beings."
3. Three main themes of continental philosophy—existentialism, phenomenology, and deconstruction—arguably all have their roots in him.
4. Heidegger's word for the "being of humans," *Dasein*, (literal meaning: "to be there") has a central place in *Being and Time*. Division one is entitled "Preparatory Fundamental Analysis of Dasein" and division two is entitled "Dasein and Temporality."
5. His association with National Socialism and membership in the Nazi party have been used by his critics to dismiss him. Conversely, his supporters have more or less dismissed this association as irrelevant to his philosophical accomplishment.[56]

MAJOR WORKS:

Being and Time
Letter on Humanism
Introduction to Metaphysics

---

56. On this point, two essays are important: Hannah Arendt, "Heidegger at Eighty" and Karsten Harries, "Heidegger as Political Thinker." Both are in Michael Murray, ed., *Heidegger and Modern Philosophy*.

WHAT TO BUY:

Heidegger, Martin. *Being and Time*. Translated by John Macquarrie and Edward Robinson. New York: Harper & Row, 1962.

Heidegger, Martin. *Martin Heidegger: Basic Writings*. Edited with General Introduction by David Farrell Krell. New York: Harper & Row, 1977.

Biemel, Walter. *Martin Heidegger: An Illustrated Study*. Translated by J. L. Mehta. New York: Harcourt Brace Jovanovich, 1976. With a figure as controversial as Heidegger, it is always important to start with someone who is sympathetic and fair. This book is as good a place to start as any.

Guignon, C., ed. *The Cambridge Companion to Heidegger*. Cambridge: Cambridge University Press, 1993.

Murray, Michael, ed. *Heidegger and Modern Philosophy*. New Haven, CT: Yale University Press, 1978. Though many more recent essays have been written on Heidegger, this book is still essential for any serious student.

WITTGENSTEIN (1889–1951)

"Wittgenstein's reputation among twentieth-century thinkers is . . . unsurpassed. His characterization as a genius is unchallenged; he has joined the philosophical canon. A poll of professional philosophers in 1998 put him fifth in a list of those who had made the most important contributions to the subject, after Aristotle, Plato, Kant, and Nietzsche and ahead of Hume and Descartes."[57]

Life Chronology:

- 1889 Born in Vienna, Austria into a large and wealthy Jewish family.
- 1908 Enrolled as a student at University of Manchester where he designed an airplane engine.
- 1911 Visited the mathematician Gottlob Frege (1848–1925) at Jena who advised him to study under Bertrand Russell at Cambridge University.
- 1912–13 Enrolled as student at Cambridge and spent five terms there.
- 1913 Went to live in Norway where he built a hut and lived by himself until outbreak of World War I.
- 1914 Served as volunteer in Austrian artillery; repeatedly decorated for bravery.
- 1918 Taken prisoner by the Italian army. He completed his *Tractatus-Logico Philosophicus* just prior to his capture and sent a copy from his prison camp to Bertrand Russell.

---

57. Edmonds and Eidinow, *Wittgenstein's Poker*, 292.

1919 Met with Russell in Holland to discuss the *Tractatus*.

1919 Returned to Vienna. He gave away his large fortune he inherited from his father to his sisters, and enrolled in a teachers' training college.

1920–26 Worked as a schoolteacher in rural Austria.

1926–28 Worked as a monastery gardener and designed a house for his sister in Vienna.

1929 Returned to Cambridge and submitted the *Tractatus* as his PhD dissertation. He was granted the degree following an oral examination by Russell and G. E. Moore. He became a research fellow at Cambridge.

1930 Began giving lectures to students at Cambridge.

1935 Visited the Soviet Union, then returned to Norway where he lived another year in his hut.

1937 Returned to Cambridge and became a British citizen when Austria was annexed by Germany.

1939 Appointed Professor of Philosophy at Cambridge but volunteered as a medical orderly when World War II began.

1945 Returned to Cambridge to teach, but resigned in 1947.

1948 Completed his *Philosophical Investigations* while living in Dublin, Ireland.

1949 Lived as a guest of Norman Malcolm, a professor at Cornell University. He returned to England when he discovered he had cancer.

1951 Died in Cambridge after spending the last two years of his life working on what was later published as *On Certainty*.

FAMOUS BECAUSE:

1. He wrote the *Tractatus-Logico Philosophicus*, a brief but highly technical work, which he later thought was mistaken in some matters.[58]
2. He urged that an analogy existed between playing games and using language, which he referred to as "language games."[59]
3. He suggested that a useful way to understand similarities between games and similarities between numbers (and by implication other things as well) was through the concept of "family resemblance."[60]
4. He proposed an argument against the possibility of "private languages."[61]
5. He wrote the posthumously published and highly influential *Philosophical Investigations* and *On Certainty*.

MAJOR WORKS:

Tractatus-Logico Philosophicus

---

58. In his preface to *Philosophical Investigations*, Wittgenstein said "I have been forced to recognize grave mistakes in what I wrote in that first book." However, see the very useful chapter entitled "The Continuity of Wittgenstein's Philosophy" in Anthony Kenny, *Wittgenstein*, 219–32.

59. Wittgenstein, *Philosophical Investigations*, section 7 and 65ff.

60. Ibid., sections 65–88.

61. Ibid., sections 243–363.

Philosophical Investigations
On Certainty

WHAT TO BUY:

Probably the most accessible of Wittgenstein's writings is *On Certainty*. Edited by G. H. von Wright. Chicago: University of Chicago Press, 1977. But I also recommend looking at *Culture and Value*. Edited by G. H. von Wright. Chicago: University of Chicago Press, 1977, before plunging into the *Philosophical Investigations*. Translated by G. E. M. Anscombe. New York: Macmillan Publishing Co, 1968.

Kenny, Anthony. *Wittgenstein*. Cambridge, MA: Harvard University Press, 1981. A number of books on Wittgenstein are worth reading, but Kenny writes in such a clear and understandable style that I recommend his book be read before any other secondary literature.

Sluga, Hans D., and David G. Stern, eds. *The Cambridge Companion to Wittgenstein*. Cambridge: Cambridge University Press, 1996.

Edmonds, David, and John Eidinow. *Wittgenstein's Poker: The Story of a Ten-Minute Argument Between Two Great Philosophers*. New York: HarperCollins, 2001. Anyone interested in Wittgenstein will want to read this book.

Bibliography

Adams, Robert M. *The Virtue of Faith and Other Essays in Philosophical Theology*. New York: Oxford University Press, 1987.

———. "A Modified Divine Command Theory of Ethical Wrongness." In *The Virtue of Faith and Other Essays in Philosophical Theology*, 97–122. New York: Oxford University Press, 1987.

———. "Idealism Vindicated." In *Persons: Human and Divine*. Edited by Peter van Inwagen and Dean Zimmerman. 35–54. Oxford: Clarendon, 2007.

Alston, W. P. *A Realist Conception of Truth*. Ithaca, NY: Cornell University Press, 1996.

Anselm of Canterbury. *Anselm of Canterbury: The Major Works*. Edited with an Introduction by Brian Davies and G. R. Evans. Oxford: Oxford University Press, 2008.

———. *St. Anselm: Basic Writings*. 2nd ed. Translated by S. N. Deane. Introduction by Charles Hartshorne. La Salle, IL: Open Court, 1990.

Ammerman, Robert R., ed. *Classics of Analytic Philosophy*. Indianapolis: Hackett, 1990.

Aquinas, Thomas. *Summa Theologiae*. 3 Vols. Translated by The Fathers of the Dominican Province. New York: Benzinger Brothers, 1947.

———. *Summa Contra Gentiles*. Notre Dame: University of Notre Dame Press, 1975.

———. *The Treatise on Law* (Being *Summa Theologiae*, I–II, QQ 90–97). Edited with an Introduction, Latin Text, Translation, and Commentary by R. J. Henle. Notre Dame: University of Notre Dame Press, 1993.

Arendt, Hannah. "Martin Heidegger at Eighty." In *Heidegger and Modern Philosophy*, edited by Michael Murray, 239–303. New Haven, CT: Yale University Press, 1978.

Aristotle. *Complete Works of Aristotle: The Revised Oxford Translation.* Edited by J. Barnes. 2 vols. Princeton, NJ: Princeton University Press, 1983.

——. *Nichomachaen Ethics.* In *Complete Works of Aristotle: The Revised Oxford Translation*, edited by J. Barnes. Vol. 2, 1729–1867. Princeton, NJ: Princeton University Press, 1983.

——. *Aristotle: Selections.* Translated with an Introduction, Notes, and Glossary by Terence Irwin and Gail Fine. Indianapolis: Hackett, 1995.

Ashley, Maurice. *England in the Seventeenth Century: The Pelican History of England: 6.* Baltimore, MD: Penguin, 1967.

Audi, Robert, ed. *The Cambridge Dictionary of Philosophy.* 2nd ed. Cambridge: Cambridge University Press, 2001.

——. *Practical Reasoning.* New York: Routledge, Chapman and Hall, 1991.

Audi, Robert, and William J. Wainwright, eds. *Rationality, Religious Belief & Moral Commitment.* Ithaca, NY: Cornell University Press, 1986.

Augustine. *Augustine: Confessions and Enchiridion.* Translated and edited by Albert C. Outler. Philadelphia: Westminster Press, 1955.

——. *Concerning the City of God Against the Pagans.* Translated by Henry Bettenson. Introduction by John O'Meara. New York: Penguin, 1984.

Biemel, Walter. *Martin Heidegger: An Illustrated Study.* Translated by J. L. Mehta. New York: Harcourt Brace Jovanovich, 1976.

Bennett, Jonathan. *Kant's Analytic.* Cambridge: Cambridge University Press, 1966.

——. *Kant's Dialectic.* Cambridge: Cambridge University Press, 1974.

Berkeley, George. *Three Dialogues Between Hylas and Philonous.* Indianapolis: Bobbs–Merill, 1954.

Boethius. *The Theological Tractates; The Consolation of Philosophy.* Translated by H. F. Stewart, E. K. Rand, and S. J. Tester. Loeb Classical Library, 74. Cambridge, MA: Harvard University Press, 1997.

Bradley, F. H. *Appearance and Reality: A Metaphysical Essay.* Oxford: Clarendon, 1966.

Carroll, Lewis. *Through the Looking Glass.* London: The Folio Society, 1962.

Chisholm, R. M. "The Problem of the Criterion." In *The Theory of Knowledge: Classical and Contemporary Readings.* 2nd ed. Edited by L. P. Pojman, 26–34. Belmont, CA: Wadsworth, 1999.

Cicero. *De Re Publica, De Legibus.* Translated by Clinton W. Keyes. Loeb Classical Library, 213. Cambridge, MA: Harvard University Press, 1961.

Cooper, John M., ed. *Plato: Complete Works.* Indianapolis: Hackett, 1997.

Copi, Irving M. and Carl Cohen. *Introduction to Logic.* 9th ed. New York: Macmillan,1994.

Copleston, F. C. *Aquinas.* Baltimore, MD: Penguin, 1959.

Dancy, Jonathan and Ernest Sosa, eds. *A Companion to Epistemology.* Oxford: Blackwell, 1992.

Descartes, Rene. *Discourse on Method, Meditations on the First Philosophy, The Principles of Philosophy.* New York: Barnes & Noble, 2004.

Durant, Will. *The Story of Civilization: The Life of Greece.* Vol. 2. New York: Simon & Schuster, 1966.

———. *The Story of Civilization: The Age of Reason.* Vol. 7. New York: Simon & Schuster, 1966.

Edmonds, David and John Eidinow. *Wittgenstein's Poker: The Story of a Ten-Minute Argument Between Two Great Philosophers.* New York: HarperCollins, 2001.

Edwards, Paul, ed. *The Encyclopedia of Philosophy.* 8 vols. New York: Macmillan, 1967.

Findlay, J. N. *Hegel: A Re-Examination.* New York: Oxford University Press, 1976.

Finnis, John. *Natural Law and Natural Rights.* Oxford: Clarendon, 1992.

Flew, Antony. *An Introduction to Western Philosophy: Ideas and Argument from Plato to Popper.* London: Thames and Hudson, 1991.

———. *There is a God.* New York: HarperCollins, 2007.

Frankena, William. *Ethics*. 2nd ed. Englewood Cliffs, NJ: Prentice-Hall, 1973.

———. "On Defining and Defending Natural Law." In *Law and Philosophy: A Symposium*, edited by Sidney Hook. New York: New York University Press, 1964.

Fumerton, Richard A. *Realism and the Correspondence Theory of Truth*. Lanham, MD: Rowman & Littlefield, 2002.

Gettier, Edmund. "Is Justified True Belief Knowledge?" *Analysis* 23 (1963) 121–123. This article has been widely anthologized. See for example, Roth, M. D. and L. Galis. eds. *Knowing*. 35–38. New York: Random House, 1970.

Gilson, Etienne. *History of Christian Philosophy in the Middle Ages*. New York: Random House, 1955.

Goodman, Nelson. *Of Mind and Other Matters*. Cambridge, MA: Harvard University Press, 1984.

Grayling, A. C., ed. *Philosophy 1: A Guide Through the Subject*. Oxford: Oxford University Press, 2001.

———, ed. *Philosophy 2: Further Through the Subject*. Oxford: Oxford University Press, 2001.

———. *Life, Sex and Ideas*. New York: Oxford University Press, 2003.

Grice, H. P. and P. F. Strawson. "In Defense of a Dogma." In *Classics of Analytic Philosophy*, edited by Robert R. Ammerman, 340–52. Indianapolis: Hackett, 1990.

Harries, Karsten. "Heidegger as a Political Thinker." In *Heidegger and Modern Philosophy*, edited by Michael Murray, 304–329. New Haven, CT: Yale University Press, 1978.

Heidegger, Martin. *Martin Heidegger: Basic Writings*. Edited by David Farrell Krell. New York: Harper & Row, 1977.

———. *Being and Time*. Translated by John Macquarrie and Edward Robinson. New York: Harper & Row, 1962.

———. *Introduction to Metaphysics*. Translated by Ralph Manheim. New York: Doubleday-Anchor, 1961.

Herodotus. *The Landmark Herodotus: The Histories*. Edited by Robert B. Strassler. Translated by Andrea L. Purvis. New York: Pantheon, 2007.

Hobbes, Thomas. *Leviathan*. Edited by Richard Tuck. Cambridge: Cambridge University Press, 1991.

Hohfeld, Wesley Newcomb. *Fundamental Legal Conceptions.* New Haven, CT: Yale University Press, 1919.

Honderich, Ted. *How Free Are You? The Determinism Problem.* New York: Oxford University Press, 1993.

———. *The Oxford Guide to Philosophy.* 2nd ed. Cambridge: Cambridge University Press, 2005.

Hume, David. *A Treatise of Human Nature.* Edited with an Introduction by Ernest C. Mossner. London: Penguin, 1984.

James, William. *The Meaning of Truth: A Sequel to "Pragmatism."* New York: Longmans Green, 1909.

Jones, Judy and William Wilson. *An Incomplete Education.* New York: Ballantine, 1987.

Kagan, Donald. *The Peloponnesian War.* New York: Penguin, 2004.

Kant, Immanuel. *Immanuel Kant's Critique of Pure Reason.* Translated by Norman Kemp Smith. New York: St. Martins, 1965.

———. *Grounding for the Metaphysics of Morals.* Translated by James Ellington. Indianapolis: Hackett, 1981.

———. *Prolegomena to Any Future Metaphysics.* Translated by Lewis White Beck. Indianapolis: Bobbs-Merrill, 1950.

———. *Kant: Selections.* Translated and edited by Lewis White Beck. New York: Scribner/Macmillan, 1988.

Katz, Jerrold J. "Analyticity." In *A Companion to Epistemology*, edited by Jonathan Dancy and Ernest Sosa, 11–17. Oxford: Blackwell, 1992.

Kenny, Anthony. *The God of the Philosophers.* Oxford: Oxford University Press, 1992.

———. *Wittgenstein.* Cambridge, MA: Harvard University Press, 1981.

———, ed. *The Oxford Illustrated History of Western Philosophy.* Oxford: Oxford University Press, 2001.

Korner, Stephen. *Kant.* New Haven, CT: Yale University Press, 1955.

Kripke, Saul A. *Naming and Necessity.* Cambridge, MA: Harvard University Press, 1998.

Kretzmann, Norman, Anthony Kenny, Jan Pinborg, Eleonore Stump, eds. *The Cambridge History of Later Medieval Philosophy.* New York: Cambridge University Press, 1989.

Laertius, Diogenes. *Lives of the Eminent Philosophers*. 2 vols. Translated by R. D. Hicks. Loeb Classical Library. 184 and 185. Cambridge, MA: Harvard University Press, 1972.

Lewis, C. S., appendix to *The Abolition of Man*. New York: Macmillan, 1955.

Locke, John. *An Essay Concerning Human Understanding*. Oxford: Clarendon, 1924.

———. *Two Treatises of Government*. Edited with introduction and notes by Peter Laslett. Cambridge: Cambridge University Press, 1988.

McInerny, Ralph. *A First Glance at St. Thomas Aquinas*. Notre Dame: University of Notre Dame Press, 1990.

MacIntyre, Alisdair. *After Virtue: A Study in Moral Theory*. 2nd ed. Notre Dame: Notre Dame University Press, 1984.

Martinich, A. P. and David Sosa, eds. *A Companion to Analytic Philosophy*. Malden, MA: Blackwell, 2001.

Mavrodes, George. "Religion and the Queerness of Morality." In Robert Audi and William J. Wainwright, eds. *Rationality, Religious Belief and Moral Commitment*. 213–226. Ithaca, NY: Cornell University Press, 1986.

Merricks, Trenton. *Truth and Ontology*. Oxford: Clarendon, 2009.

Mill, John Stuart. *Utilitarianism*. Edited by Oskar Piest. New York: Macmillan, 1989.

Murray, Michael, ed. *Heidegger and Modern Philosophy*. New Haven, CT: Yale University Press, 1978.

Pike, Nelson. "Divine Omniscience and Voluntary Action." In Michael Peterson, William Hasker, Bruce Reichenbach, and David Basinger, eds. *Philosophy of Religion: Selected Readings*. 3rd ed. 149–155. New York: Oxford University Press, 2007.

Plato. *The Republic of Plato*. 2nd ed. Translated with notes and interpretive essay by Allan Bloom. New York: Basic Books, 1991.

Plantinga, Alvin. "Justification in the 20th Century." *Philosophy and Phenomenological Research*. Fall, 1990 Vol. L. Supplement: 45–71.

———. "How to Be an Anti-Realist." *Proceedings and Addresses of the American Philosophical Society*, Vol. 56, No. 1 (September 1982): 47–70.

———. "De Essentia." In *Essays in the Metaphysics of Modality*. Edited by Matthew Davidson. 139157. New York: Oxford University Press, 2003.

———. *God, Freedom, and Evil*. Grand Rapids, MI: Eerdmans, 1974.

Plutarch. *The Lives of the Noble Grecians and Romans*. Translated by John Dryden. Great Books of the Western World, vol. 14. Chicago: Encyclopaedia Britanica, Inc., 1952.

Polkinghorne, John. *The Faith of a Physicist*. Minneapolis: Fortress, 1996.

Quinn, Philip L. "The Recent Revival of Divine Command Ethics." *Philosophy and Phenomenological Research* Vol. L, Supplement, (Fall 1990): 345–365.

Quinn, Philip L. and Charles Taliaferro. *A Companion to Philosophy of Religion*. Malden, MA: Blackwell, 1999.

Quine, Willard Van Orman. "On What There Is." In *From a Logical Point of View: Nine Logico-Philosophical Essays*. 2nd ed. 1–19. New York: Harper Torchbooks, 1961.

———. "Two Dogmas of Empiricism." In *From a Logical Point of View: Nine Logico-Philosophical Essays*. 2nd ed. 20–46. New York: Harper Torchbooks, 1961.

Quine, W. V. and Ullian, J. S. *The Web of Belief*. 2nd ed. New York: Random House, 1978.

Reid, Thomas. *Essays on the Intellectual Powers of Man: A Critical Edition*. Edited by Derek R. Brookes. Annotations by Derek R. Brookes and Knud Haakonssen. University Park: The Pennsylvania State University Press, 2002.

Rescher, Nicholas. "How Wide is the Gap Between Facts and Values?"*Philosophy and Phenomenological Research,* vol. L, Supplement, (Fall 1990): 297–319.

Rorty, Richard. *Philosophy and the Mirror of Nature*. Princeton, NJ: Princeton University Press, 1979.

Ross, David. *Aristotle*. Introduction by J. L. Ackrill. New York: Routledge, 1995.

Russell, Bertrand. *History of Western Philosophy*. London: The Folio Society, 2004.

Singer, Peter, ed. *A Companion to Ethics*. Oxford: Blackwell, 1993.

Scruton, Roger. *Modern Philosophy*. New York: Allen Lane Penguin, 1994.

———. *From Descartes to Wittgenstein: A Short History of Modern Philosophy*. New York: Harper Torchbooks, 1981.

Smith, Huston. *The World's Religions*. San Francisco: HarperSanFrancisco, 1991.

Smith, Peter. *An Introduction to Formal Logic*. Cambridge: Cambridge University Press, 2003.

Swinburne, Richard. *The Evolution of the Soul*. Oxford: Clarendon, 1986.

———. *The Coherence of Theism*. Oxford: Oxford University Press, 1986.

———. *Is There a God?* rev. ed. New York: Oxford University Press, 2010.

Taylor, Richard. *Ethics, Faith, and Reason*. Englewood Cliffs, NJ: Prentice-Hall, 1985.

van Inwagen, Peter. *An Essay on Free Will*. Oxford: Clarendon, 1986.

———. *Metaphysics*. Boulder, CO: Westview, 1993.

Weinberg, Julius R. *A Short History of Medieval Philosophy*. Princeton, NJ: Princeton University Press, 1964.

Whitehead, Alfred North. *Process and Reality: An Essay in Cosmology*. New York: Free Press, 1978.

Wittgenstein, Ludwig. *Philosophical Investigations*. 3rd ed. Translated by G. E. M. Anscombe. New York: Macmillan, 1968.

Wolterstorff, Nicholas. "Are Concept-Users World Makers?" In *Philosophical Perspectives, Volume 1: Metaphysics 1987*. Edited by James E. Tomberlin. 233–267. Atascadero, CA: Ridgeview, 1987.

Xenephon. *Conversations of Socrates*. Translated by Hugh Tredennick and Robin Waterfield. London: Penguin, 1990.

Subject/Name Index

A

Academy, 89, 92
accidental, 48–49
Adams, Marilyn, 39fn4
Adams, Robert, 44fn18, 72–72
Alexander (the Great), 92, 93
Albert the Great, 102
Alston, William, 29fn16
Ambrose, 96
analytic, 26–27
    geometry, 107
Annicerius of Cyrene, 88
Anselm, 99–101
Aosta, Italy, 99
a posteriori, 25
a priori, 25
Aquinas, 62, 64, 73fn38, 102–105
Arendt, Hannah, 122
Arginusae, Battle of, 85, 88
argument, 6
Aristophenes, 86
Aristotle, 14, 15, 31fn20, 39–40, 54, 62, 64, 69–70, 89, 90, 92–95, 103, 104, 121
Athens, 85, 86, 87, 88, 89, 92, 93
atonement, 101
Audi, Robert, 17
Augustine, 62, 64, 96–98
Austen, Jane, 108fn38
Austerlitz
Ayer, A.J., 79

B

Babylon, 93
Bari, Council of, 100
Battle of Hastings, 99
Bec, 99
belief, 20–21
Bennett, Jonathan, 84
Berkeley, George, 41fn11, 42–44
Berlin, University of, 119
Bloom, Alan, 89fn17
body, 44–45
Boethius, 52fn34
Bradley, F. H., 28fn12
Brandenburg, 110
Bristol, England, 110
Buddhism, 60
Bultmann, Rudolf, 122
Bush, George H.W., 9
Bush, George W., 9

C

Cambridge, University of, 78, 126, 127
Categories, 39
categorical imperative, 116
cause,
    efficient, 55
    final, 55
    formal, 54
    material, 54

Cerularius, Michael, 99
Chalcidice peninsula (Chalcis), 92, 93
Charles I, 107, 110
chemistry, 2
chimpanzee (chimp), 4, 18–19, 56–57
Chisholm, Roderick, 81, 82fn9
Christianity, 44, 60
Christina of Sweden (Queen), 107
Cicero, 64, 65, 96
Clinton, Bill, 9
compatibilism, 52–53
conceive, 4
conclusion, 5–6
consequentialism, 67–69
contingent, 24
Cooper, Anthony Ashley (Earl of Shaftsbury), 110, 111
Copernician revolution, 116
Copleston, Frederick, 103fn33
Cornell, University of 127

D

Dasein, 82, 124
deconstruction, 80
deduction, 7–9
Delium, battle of, 85
deontology, 66–67
Derrida, Jacques, 80–81
Descartes, 45, 106–109, 116
determinism, 50–52
difference
    in degree, 56–57
    in kind, 56–57
Dion, 88
Dionysius I, 88
Dionysius II, 89
divine command ethics, 70–71

dualist, 45
Dublin, Ireland, 127
Duns Scotus, 121
duty, 66–67

E

economics, 2
eliminativist, 45
Elizabeth of Palatine (Princes), 107
empiricism, 33–34
England, 110, 111
epistemology, 20–36
essence, 46–48
essential, 48–49
ethics, 93
Euthyphro Dilemma, 71–73
evil/good, 61–64
excluded middle (law of), 15
existence, 46–48
existentialism, 80

F

faith, 101
fallacy, 12–13
    formal, 12
    informal, 12–13
family resemblance, 128
Findlay, J.N., 118fn47
Finnis, John, 74fn40
Five Ways, 104
Flew, Antony, 62–63
Fossanova, 103
Frankena, William, 64, 69fn28
French Revolution, 118
freedom (significant), 51
free will, 50–52

Frege, Gottlob, 126
Freiburg, University of, 121, 122, 123
Fumerton, Richard, 29fn16

G

Gadamer, Hans-Georg, 122
Gettier, Edmund, 22
Glorious Revolution, 111
Grayling, A.C., 63
Great Schism, 99
Greek philosophy, 44
Gregory X (Pope), 103
God, 49, 51, 62, 65, 70–73, 100, 101, 116
good/evil, 61–64
Goodman, Nelson, 35fn27

H

Harold II (of England), 99
Hartshorne, Charles, 100fn30
Hegel, G.W.F, 118–120
    Hegelian idealism, 78
Heidegger, Martin, 80–82, 119, 121–124
Heidelberg, University of, 119
Henry I, 100
Hermeias, 92
Herodotus, 1
Hinduism, 60
Hippo (Annaba, Algeria), 96
Hobbes, Thomas, 65–66
Hohfeld, Wesley Newcomb, 74–76
Holland, 111
Holy Spirit, 100
humanities, xi

Hume, David, 41, 59fn1, 79, 114, 116, 117
Husserl, Edmund, 80, 122

I

idealism, 41–44, 119
    absolute, 42fn12
    subjective, 42fn12
    transcendental, 42fn12
identity (law of), 15
incompatibilism, 52–53
induction, 7–9
infer, 4
inference, 5
is/ought, 58–59
Islam, 60
Isocrates, 89fn16

J

James II, 111
James, William, 27
Jena,
    Battle of, 118
    University of, 118
Jesus of Nazareth, 1
Judaism, 60, 71

K

Kant, Immanuel, 26, 84, 114–117, 122fn53
    and anti-realism, 36
    and deontology, 66–67
Kenny, Anthony, 50fn29, 106fn34
Kierkegaard, Soren, 119
knowledge, 21–22

Knutzen, Martin 114
Konigsberg, Prussia, 114, 115
   university of 114
Kreeft, Peter, 104
Kripke, Saul, 48fn25

L

La Fleche (Jesuit college), 106
La Haye, France, 106
language games, 128
Leftow, Brian, 52fn34
Leibniz, Gottfried W., 114, 116
Lesbos, island of, 92
Lewis, C.S., 60fn3
liberal arts, xi
liberty
   of spontaneity, 50
   of indifference, 50
logic, 3, 4–19, 93, 114
logical positivism, 79
Locke, John, 26fn8, 65, 110–113, 116
Leo IX (Pope), 99
Lombard, Peter, 102
Lyon, Council of, 103

M

McInerny, Ralph, 102nf32
MacIntyre, Alisdair, 70fn31
Malcolm, Norman, 127
Manchester, University of, 126
Mani, 96fn26
Marburg, University of 122
Marx, Karl, 119
Maurice of Nassau, 106
Mavrodes, George, 67fn25
mathematics, 35

Meletus, 86
Merricks, Trenton, 30, 31fn21
Messkirch, Germany, 121
metaphysics, 3, 37–57, 93, 114
Mill, John Stuart, 67–68
mind, 44–45
Monte Casino, 102
Moore, G.E., 78
moral philosophy/ethics, 3, 58–77, 110

N

Naples, University of, 103
Napoleon, 118
National Socialism, 122, 124
natural law, 64–66
natural philosophy, 2
Nazi party, 122, 123, 124
necessary, 16–17, 24,
necessary truth, 73
necessity, 7–8, 12
Nichomachean Ethics, 62fn8, 64fn15, 94
non-contradiction (law of), 14
Norman invasion, 99
Norway, 126, 127

O

Obama, Barrack, 9
Ockham (Occam), 39
ontological argument, 100
Order of Preachers (Dominicans), 102

P

Paul of Tarsus, 65
Paris, 106
Paris, University of, 102, 103
particular, 38-39
Peloponnesian War, 85-86, 88
pentateuch, 71
perceive, 4, 42
Pericles, 88
phenomenology, 80
Philip of Macedon, 92, 93
philosophy
    analytic, 78-82
    and science, 1-3
    continental, 78-82
physics, 2
Pike, Nelson, 51fn32
Plantinga, Alvin., 22fn3, 35fn27, 48fn25, 51fn30
Plato, 14, 39, 61-62, 64fn14, 71, 85, 87fn10, 88-91, 92, 93, 97, 122fn53
Plutarch, 93fn21
Poiters, University of, 106
political philosophy, 93
Polkinghorne, John, 28fn14
Potidaea, 85
premise, 5-6
private languages, 128
probability, 7
property, 39-41
    accidental, 48-49
    essential, 40, 47, 48-49
    necessary, 46-47
Proslogion, 99, 101fn31
Protestant, 81, 106
Pythagorean School of Crotona, 89fn16
Pythias, 92, 93

Q

Quine, W.V.O., 20fn1, 21fn2, 27fn9, 37
Quinn, Philip, 71fn33

R

rationalism, 33-34
realism
    and anti-realism, 34-36
    and idealism, 41-44
reasoning,
    practical, 17-19
    theoretical, 17-19
rhetoric, 93, 96, 110
Rescher, Nicholas, 59fn2
Reid, Thomas, 43-44
Republic, 64fn6, 90
right/wrong, 60-61
rights, 74-77
Roccasecca, Naples, 102
Rome 100, 103
Roman Catholic, 81, 104, 106, 121
Rorty, Richard, 30fn17
Roscelin (Roscellinus) 99
Russell, Bertrand, 2fn4, 78-79, 126

S

Santa Claus, 46
Sartre, Jean Paul, 81
satisfaction (theory of), 101
science (modern sense), 2
    and philosophy, 1-3
Scruton, Roger, 43fn14
Seusippus, 92
skepticism, 97

Socrates, 8, 84fn1, 85–87, 88, 90
sound (soundness), 11–12
Soviet Union, 127
Stagira, 92, 93
Strauss, Leo, 122
Stuttgart, Wurttemberg, 118
substance, 39–41
sufficient, 16–17
supervene/supervenience, 61
Swinburne, Richard, 73
synthetic, 26–27

T

Taylor, Richard, 67fn25
ten commandments, 71
Thagaste, 96
Thales of Miletus, 1
Thirty Years War, 106
truth, (theories of)
    coherence, 28–29
    correspondence, 29–31, 31–33
    pragmatic, 27
    realist, 31–33
Tubingen, University of, 118

U

universal, 38–39
utilitarianism, 67–69

V

valid (validity), 9–11
van Inwagen, Peter, 23fn6, 34fn26, 48fn26, 51fn31, 53fn36
Vandals, 96
Vienna, Austria, 126, 127
    Vienna Circle, 79

virtue ethics, 69–70

W

Weinberg, Julius, 96fn25, 97fn27
Wolterstorff, Nicholas, 35fn27
wrong/right, 60–61
William the Conqueror, 99
William II, 100
William III, 111
Wittgenstein, Ludwig, 79, 126–129
Wolff, Christian, 114, 116

X

Xenophon, 85, 87, 90fn19

www.ingramcontent.com/pod-product-compliance
Lightning Source LLC
Chambersburg PA
CBHW072142160426
43197CB00012B/2212